THE ASTORS:

AN AMERICAN LEGEND

Other Books by Lucy Kavaler

THE ASTORS, *a Family Chronicle of Pomp and Power*

MUSHROOMS, MOLDS, AND MIRACLES

THE PRIVATE WORLD OF HIGH SOCIETY

For Young Readers

DANGEROUS AIR

THE WONDERS OF FUNGI

THE ARTIFICIAL WORLD AROUND US

THE WONDERS OF ALGAE

THE
ASTORS
An American Legend

LUCY KAVALER

ILLUSTRATED

DODD, MEAD & COMPANY

NEW YORK

Library of Congress Catalog Card Number: 68-8283
Printed in the United States of America
by The Cornwall Press, Inc., Cornwall, N. Y.

For
Blanche and Max Kavaler

Contents

Illustrations

Illustrations

THE ASTORS:

AN AMERICAN LEGEND

1

John Jacob Astor
and the Making of a Fortune

IT WAS A CITY different in every way from the modern idea of what a city should be. There were no police, no firemen, no street lights, no street cleaners, no running water, and no public transportation. This was the New York that greeted young John Jacob Astor on his arrival in the year 1784.

Thieves—and there were many in those lawless years—had only to wait until the night watchman had gone by with his cry of ". . . o'clock and all's well."

If a man did not own a horse and carriage, he walked, and walking in New York of the 1780's was not easy for the old or the weak. Planks were thrown over the ditches that pitted the dirt paths. Anyone who ventured more than a few hundred yards from his house had to make his way through swamps, woods, and open fields, or circle around cabbage farms and wheatfields. What is now downtown New York was a pleasant, sleepy countryside with little ponds, lofty trees, rolling hills, and a scattering of farmhouses and church steeples. In order to go to Brooklyn, one had to get a boat and row across the river.

The dirt throughout the city was utterly disgusting. Pigs rooted around in the stinking, rotting garbage that lay in the streets of even the best neighborhoods. Dust, ashes, leaves, and manure from horses and pigs were pushed into the middle of the crude streets and left there. After a rainstorm women trailed their skirts through rivers of foul-smelling mud. Cleanliness in a city without running water was a luxury for the rich only. Rain, collected in buckets left out on the rooftops, was used for washing clothes and bathing. There was no reservoir, so housewives had to run to the public pumps at the street corners for their drinking water. The best-tasting water came from the "Tea Water Pump," located in what was to become the business district. For years it was peddled through the streets in casks labeled "tea water—2¢ a pail."

Still, if one tries to see New York through Astor's eyes, it was a crowded, immense, exciting city, full of opportunity. The Revolutionary War had just ended and Americans were filled with pride and the desire to make more of their young country and of this city. This attitude was matched by the boundless ambition of John Jacob Astor. New York was his natural spiritual home. The combination of the man, the time, and the place was right; Astor needed America to fulfill himself and the young growing country needed men like him.

His story began on June 17, 1763, in the small German village of Walldorf where his father ran the local butcher shop. John's mother died when he was small and his father married again. There were twelve children of the two marriages in the home, but it was not a happy one. His stepmother, like those in fairy tales, could not stand the children of the first wife and made John and his brothers and sisters miserable. His schooling came to an end when he was fourteen, because his father could not see why any healthy boy should be indulged with lessons when he was big enough to work. For the rest of his life, John was unable to write the simplest letter without making mistakes in spelling and punctuation. Instead of learning, he slaved all day with stinking carcasses in the butcher shop and returned at night to a dark and loveless house.

Two of John's older brothers, equally unhappy, left home to search for a better life. George went to England and Henry to New York. By the time John was seventeen, he decided that he, too, could stand it no more. He wanted to go to America right away, but the American Revolution was being fought and he could not obtain passage on a ship. Instead he went to England and was put to work in his brother George's music store. John learned a lot about music and took up the flute. But he was not content in England and as soon as the War ended, made his way across the ocean to America.

John was welcomed to New York by his brother

Henry, who was running a meat stall in Fulton Market. But Henry was more than just a butcher and made extra money by investing his earnings in real estate. Henry was willing to employ his younger brother, but John had not left Walldorf to become a butcher in New York. There were clearly many jobs available for a strong young man. He saw porters standing with wheelbarrows at the street corners, offering to carry a load above Chambers Street for $12\frac{1}{2}$ cents and below for $18\frac{3}{4}$ cents. Surely he could do better than that.

Astor was soon hired to peddle a heavy tray of cakes and cookies through the pitted streets of New York. His next job sounds even worse—beating the dust and bugs out of furs and then packing them into bales. The work brought him two dollars a week and meals. It would have been repulsive to anyone not used to the bad smells, blood, and mess of a butcher shop, but Astor saw it as a stepping stone to the glorious future he never for a moment doubted was to be his.

Robert Bowne, his employer, sent John into the wild country north of Albany to trade with the Indians. He struggled through the forests on foot, carrying on his back a pack with his supplies and the cheap cloth, tobacco, and bright jewelry that the Indians would accept as payment for their beaver, otter, and muskrat skins. The trip back was even more difficult, as the neat pack was replaced by bundles of foul-smelling animal pelts. Other traders warned him that death was always near at hand. If he were to wander off the poorly marked trails, he might stumble into territory occupied by hostile Indians. But John Jacob was not a man to worry about what might happen. He enjoyed bargaining with the Indians, getting them to give him their valuable furs for practically nothing.

John came back from these wanderings to his room in Widow Todd's boardinghouse. The daughter, Sarah, who helped with the housework, was a slender girl, with great big eyes in a thin face. And before long John asked her to marry him. Although Mrs. Todd was not rich, she had saved three hundred dollars for a dowry for Sarah. Astor used the money, the largest sum he had possessed until then, to open an odd little store where he sold not only pianos and flutes, but also the furs that were to make him famous.

Still, he did not marry Sarah for her money. Long afterward one of their grandchildren asked him why he had married Sarah, who had become a strict and cross old lady. John Jacob thought for a moment and answered: "Because she was so pretty."

No one ever said anything similar about him. John was not handsome, with his big nose and small piercing eyes beneath heavy eyebrows. Although he was five feet, nine inches tall, a good height for a man of the eighteenth century, his square, stocky build made him look shorter. And he was fat before he was middle-aged. But his looks were never the important thing about him. The man was so full of life that it was exciting to be in his presence.

When first married, the young couple worked together as a team, living modestly in rooms right over the store. Sarah was quite capable of taking charge of the shop while her husband went out to trade for furs. She was even better able than he to judge the quality of furs, and he knew it. In later years he would ask her for an opinion when a particularly important fur sale was being considered. Sarah would study the furs and quietly tell him what they were worth. Then she charged him five hundred dollars an hour for her services. It was a strange thing for a wife to do, but John only laughed and paid her.

He journeyed to upper New York State and on into Canada, as he had done when working for Mr. Bowne. It seemed to him that there was a fortune to be made in furs. Most of North America was still a wilderness through which roamed millions upon millions of animals. An energetic trader could obtain countless beaver, otter, seal, and muskrat skins from the Indians. And he could sell every one easily in a period when houses were poorly heated and traveling was done on foot or in chilly horse-drawn carriages.

One might think that other men would have seen the same opportunity, but *no* other American exploited the fur trade in the way that John Jacob did. The business was simply too repulsive, dirty, and dangerous to appeal to gentlemen born to wear clean linen and shoes with silver buckles. Rich men hired others to do their trading for them, but this was not as effective as dealing with Indians and white trappers personally. Most men were also put off by the difficulties of operating a fur business. The British, angry at having been defeated by their former colonists, tried to keep the Americans from making profits on furs. They insisted that any furs bought in British territory, which included Montreal in Canada and most frontier posts, had to be shipped to London and only then sent back to New York.

None of this bothered Astor. He was no gentleman. If there was money to be made, he would make it, no matter how difficult, strenuous, or repulsive the work involved might be. He had staggered beneath a heavy pack for Bowne's benefit; he would do it for his own. As an experienced trader, he could get furs from the Indians so cheaply that even after sending them to London and back, he could still make a good profit on each skin.

In fact, he made so much money that he decided to invest some of it. His brother Henry gave him a piece of good advice: buy land. Furs were still John's main interest; he did not yet realize how valuable real estate would become.

Forty years were to pass before Astor was to say wistfully: "Could I begin life again, knowing what I now know and had money to invest, I would buy every foot of land on the island of Manhattan."

While the Astor fortune was growing, so was his family. Though she ran the shop with quiet efficiency downstairs, Sarah still managed to bear eight children upstairs. Five of them lived, a fairly good record for the period. Three years after giving birth to a daughter, Magdalen, Sarah produced the eagerly awaited son, John Jacob Astor II. It soon became clear, however, that something was very wrong with the boy. Written accounts of the time do not make clear whether he was retarded or insane. His wild moods and inability to learn saddened his parents. John Jacob I never gave up hope that the boy would one day become normal. He insisted that the brothers and sisters treat little John as if nothing were wrong with him, an obviously impossible demand.

But Astor was not to be cheated of his heir. William Backhouse Astor was born in 1792 to carry on the Astor name and in time the family fortune. Two daughters, Dorothea and Eliza, followed. Astor was a warm, loving, even doting father, but his personality was so overpowering that he dominated his children completely. "Father knows best" was the policy of the home, and at least in terms of building a fortune, it was the right one. It has often been said that the Astors made and kept more money for longer than any other family in American history. The statement is true, but incomplete. The Astors made and kept this money, because the children and grandchildren dutifully followed the orders of John Jacob I.

Astor relied principally on hard work to raise himself from rags to riches and he was shrewd enough to seize every opportunity that presented itself. In 1794 statesman John Jay negotiated a treaty with Great Britain that allowed traders to send furs directly from Canada to New York, without first shipping them to England.

"Now I will make my fortune in the fur trade!" exclaimed Astor when he heard the news.

John Jacob Astor

Hundreds of thousands of skins passed over the border to his storeroom. John Jacob no longer traveled himself. Although he was only in his early thirties, his health had been injured by the heavy labor of his youth. He hired agents and directed their every action, just as he did those of his children. His men were sent ever deeper into the wilderness to set up trading posts where the Indians could bring the pelts of the animals they had trapped. They went to regions where no white man had ever been before.

Four years after the treaty was signed, Astor was worth a quarter of a million dollars, a tremendous fortune for 1800, a time when a whole family could live comfortably on seven hundred-and-fifty dollars a year. Unable to forget the poverty of his youth, he continued to watch every penny.

He also looked for ways of earning more. In the early years of the nineteenth century, John had a brilliant idea. Why not sell furs in China and use the money on the spot to buy silks, spices, and tea, which were scarce and valuable in America? The same ship that carried the furs to China would bring the desirable products back, and he would sell them for huge profit in New York.

No other man had attempted such a plan, because it was clearly impossible, with the British East India Company in full control of trade with the Orient. There was no reason for it to let Americans in. But the impossible was merely a challenge to Astor, who went to England and talked the company officials into giving him permission to take ships into any of its ports. No one has ever been able to explain why the British did this. It is probable that the East India Company thought Astor would fail. Selling furs to the Chinese must have struck them as similar to selling ice to the Eskimos. After all, northern China and nearby Russia both contained vast numbers of fur-bearing animals. But if any man could break into that Chinese market, Astor could do it, and he did.

He bought a share of a ship, then a whole ship, then a whole fleet of ships, and within a few years was the leading figure in the China trade. His very best furs, first checked by Sarah's trained eye, went to China. He called upon his trappers to furnish so many of the sea-otter pelts favored by the wealthy citizens of Canton and Shanghai that this breed of animal was nearly wiped out. Astor was indifferent; his profit on the silks, tea, and spices sold in America was tremendous.

Even then he was not satisfied with the fortune he was making. Discontent was a key element of his personality. It had taken him out of Walldorf and then London, had lifted him from a start as a street peddler to the possession of hundreds of thousands of dollars; and still that was not enough. There was always a way for an alert man to earn a little more. Astor's ships broke their journey at the Hawaiian Islands to take on food and water. What might Hawaii have to offer a smart businessman? It did not take John Jacob long to figure that one out. Sandalwood was plentiful there, and so he instructed his agents to buy it—cheaply, of

course—and add it to the cargo. This lovely wood became popular both here and in China and Astor's
monoply of the sandalwood trade lasted for nearly
twenty years.

During the uneasy period before the War of 1812 the
government ordered American ships to stay in New
York harbor. Astor, determined to get one ship off to
China, looked for a way around the law. A Chinese
mandarin, Punqua Wing-Chong, was found and sent to
ask Senator Samuel Mitchell of New York to let him go
home for his father's funeral. Mitchell sent a letter to
President Thomas Jefferson describing the unhappiness
of the mandarin. Jefferson kindly gave his permission
for Punqua to be taken home to China on the American
ship *Beaver*. The name alone should have been a hint
that a noted fur merchant was owner of the ship, but no
one noticed the connection until a huge cargo of fine
furs was carried on board. Astor then pointed out calmly
that it would be ridiculous to send out a big ship carrying only a single Chinese gentleman. The other mer-
chants and shipowners rushed to write letters, sign
petitions, and issue complaints. It was too late. Jefferson
had approved the sailing of the *Beaver* and sail it did . . .
and return, too, with a cargo of tea and silk and sandalwood and spices. As it was the first ship to come into
New York in more than a year, Astor was able to raise
prices on everything and earned more than $200,000
from that one voyage.

By this time Astor had become friends with some of
the most prominent men in the country. Still, his man-

ners had remained crude and boorish. At one dinner party he wiped his fingers on the sleeve of the lady seated next to him. "Oh, Mr. Astor," fluttered the hostess, "I must have forgotten to give you a serviette [napkin]." After another dinner a lady wrote: "He dined here last night and ate his ice cream and peas with a knife."

To be sure, if Astor's manners were unsuitable for high society, they were no worse than the average of the period. An etiquette book found it necessary to advise that "nothing but sheer necessity can excuse any teeth picking at the table," and it is not proper "for gentlemen to blow their noses with their fingers."

People put up with Astor's manners, not only because he was rich and successful, but also because of his fascinating personality. Astor would not have bothered to change, because he was really not much interested in social life. He might have thought differently if Sarah accompanied him to parties, but she was too shy and retiring to go out. As it was, his consuming passion remained business.

Aware that even the highly profitable China trade was based on furs, he looked for ways of increasing what was already a lion's share of the fur trade. He had been buying most of his skins in Canada, but perhaps it was time for a change. New frontiers were opening. In 1806 Captain Meriwether Lewis and William A. Clark had completed a successful government-sponsored expedition of exploration that took them from St. Louis through the Far West. Suddenly everyone was becoming aware of this immense unexplored territory. The significance of Lewis and Clark's expedition was clear to all men of vision, and Astor saw it from his own viewpoint, that of the businessman. There were fur-bearing animals in the wild country west and northwest of the Great Lakes, and he wanted them. A British-run company already dominated fur trading in the area, but Astor thrived on competition.

He founded the American Fur Company and decided to establish a fur empire—a chain of trading posts along the Missouri and Columbia rivers and the streams flowing into them. The capital, "Astoria," would be located at the mouth of the Columbia River.

Two expeditions, one by land and one by sea, were organized to make the westward journey. John's ship, the *Tonquin,* was commanded by Lieutenant Jonathan Thorn, who had been given a leave of absence from the Navy at the special request of President James Madison. Astor was so powerful that he counted even the President as a friend and Madison had made the request as a favor for Astor. It was to be the most unfortunate favor ever done him.

Thorn was a brutal and inhuman leader. Five sailors were late in getting back to the *Tonquin* from a shore expedition in the Falkland Islands, so he simply set sail without them. The men rowed frantically after the ship for three hours before being allowed back on board.

Still, he did reach the destination, the mouth of the Columbia River, and his men began to build the great Fort Astoria. The land was covered with trees and rocks, and in two months, they managed to clear only one acre. Thorn decided to leave a few men behind to work on the fort and set off to find Indians with whom to trade.

At Clayoquot Sound he invited the savage Salish Indians to bring their furs on board. Before Thorn had set out, Astor had given him a piece of advice: "Don't let too many Indians on the ship at a time." Thorn, however, never took advice, and a large party of Salish trooped on deck. The bargaining got off to a bad start. When the chief demanded a high price for the skins, Thorn hit him in the face with an otter skin.

"I fear we are in the hands of a lunatic!" exclaimed Alexander McKay, one of Astor's partners.

He pleaded with Thorn to treat the Salish in a more decent manner, but Thorn did not think Indians were human beings at all. To him, they seemed little better than animals, and so he was not suspicious when the clever Indian chief made a suggestion: "We'll give you our furs in exchange for your knives." Thorn jumped at this excellent bargain. The Indians waited until all had knives; then they turned on the white men and hacked them to pieces. Two Indian braves seized the unlucky McKay, lifted him high over their heads, and dropped him overboard. He fell into a war canoe loaded with squaws who killed him with cooking utensils. Thorn, who had been to blame for the disaster, died fighting gallantly.

The tragic news reached Astor on a night when he planned to go to the theater. He refused to change his plans. "What would you have me do?" he asked a friend who was shocked by his seeming lack of feeling. "Would you have me stay at home and weep for what I cannot help?"

The reports coming from the land expedition to Astoria were also tragic. The travelers struggling through forests and deserts endured nearly two years of unbelievable suffering and hardship. At one time they were so hungry they shot and ate their horses. Hostile Indians attacked and killed some of the men and others drowned while trying to go down a river by canoe. In 1812 a few starving, exhausted survivors staggered into Astoria, where they were greeted by those members of Thorn's party who had been lucky enough to be left behind.

As soon as they recovered their strength, they took part in the building of the trading post and fort. They made a small schooner of fir timbers and still thought kindly enough of their employer to name it the "Dolly" after one of Astor's daughters, Dorothea. The schooner sailed on Northwestern rivers, and trading posts were set up at places that later became Boise, Salem, and Spokane.

At last it looked as if Astor's dream of empire were going to become reality. And then the War of 1812 broke out. Astor tried to get a ship to Astoria in time to defend it against the British. He failed and Astoria was captured. The Union Jack was flown above the fort which Astor's men had so laboriously built.

Astor's agents at Astoria wanted no trouble and let the British North West Fur Company buy more than

$200,000 worth of furs for less than $80,500. Otter skins valued at $5.00 apiece went for $.50.

This has gone down in history as Astor's one great defeat. It was not the nature of the man to be defeated. "While I breath and so long as I have a dollar to spend I'll pursue a course to have our injuries repair'd," he wrote to a friend. "And when I am no more, I hope you'll act in my place; we have been sold, but I do not dispond." (The spelling is Astor's.)

He went on from that low point to one success after another. As for Astoria, even there his efforts were not in vain. After the war, Astoria was returned to the United States by the Treaty of Ghent. It helped to establish the American claim to the Oregon country, which became a state of the union in 1859.

Astor's private life was also upset during the war years by the elopement of his daughter Dorothea. Only seventeen-years-old and fat, she fell madly in love with penniless Colonel Walter Langdon. Her father was horrified and ordered her to come home. But Dolly, who had always before been so obedient, refused. She stayed with her husband and in time bore him eight children. For many years Astor pretended they did not exist, and then one day he went to a party at the house of a friend and saw a pretty little girl romping about merrily. Something about her face brought a lump to his throat.

"What is your name, little girl?"

"Sarah Sherburne Langdon," she lisped prettily.

He looked into her eyes and gave a deep sigh. "For

your sake, I shall have to forgive your father and your mother."

By then Astor had become so rich that he bought the Langdons an estate, Hyde Park, and supported the entire family in comfort.

Astor's setback at Astoria had caused him to stumble only once on his road to financial greatness. When the war was over, he had returned to the fur business and built up his American Fur Company. It became so powerful that if someone mentioned *the* Company, he could mean only Astor's.

His hunters, trappers, and agents helped to open the West as United States territory. Still, they must bear some of the blame for the tragedy of the American Indian. Astor's men cheated the Indians out of their furs and provided them with liquor, even though this was against the law. All the fur traders used liquor in their dealings with the Indians, but as in everything, Astor was better at it. The Indians, confused by the whisky they had drunk, lost track of fur prices. In any event, they were charged so much for the liquor and worthless merchandise being offered as barter that they were sometimes in debt to *the* Company. One year Astor reported that the Winnebagos, Sacs, and Foxes owed him $50,000, and this was at a time when a pack of beaver pelts was valued at $180.

Astor's agents and traders hired white workmen for the heavy labor and agreed to pay two hundred-and-fifty dollars for three years. The unlucky workmen did not always get even that. The labor they performed was so backbreaking that few survived for long. Their immediate employers, the traders, were kept so deeply in debt to the company by means of the high prices charged them for supplies that they sometimes had their workmen murdered when the time came to pay the wages owing.

As for Astor, he became so rich that he even lent money to President James Monroe. "It may not bee convenient to repay me the Sume Lend to you nor am I particularly in want of it," went a letter from Astor to the President. (Three years after Monroe's term ended, Astor demanded repayment, quite unmoved by the fact that the ex-President was short of money. By then, Astor was friends with the next President, John Quincy Adams.)

While Monroe was still President, Astor expected and obtained special favors. People whispered that laws all but written by Astor were regularly introduced into Congress. There was even a loophole in the liquor law, permitting whisky to be provided for "boatmen." A law barred Canadians from the American fur trade, but when John found that he needed Canadian laborers, he asked Monroe to exempt them. It appeared that the law's only aim was to keep Astor's Canadian competitors from operating here.

With such help, *the* Company took over many of the trading posts of other companies. The United States government, however, was also maintaining trading posts where the rights of the Indians were carefully guarded. Before long Senator Thomas Hart Benton of

Missouri, who just happened to be lawyer for the American Fur Company, was making speeches to Congress urging that the government get out of business. Astor brought both direct and indirect pressure to bear on other legislators, and in 1822 the government decided to close its trading posts.

John Jacob went on and on, engulfing his competitors. Soon buyers from all over the world were coming to his spring and fall auctions. On a single day, 550,000 muskrat skins were sold. When Astor finally disposed of the American Fur Company in 1834, it had earned two million dollars for him.

Furs and the China trade were not his only sources of income. During the years when he was doing what would have been a full-time job for anyone else, he was also buying all the land he could obtain.

One of his most valuable pieces of property in what is now New York's Greenwich Village came to him in a rather strange way. In 1803 Vice-President Aaron Burr fell into debt. Remembering that he had at one time lived near rising young John Jacob Astor, he asked for a loan. In return, he gave Astor 241 lots of his property. The following year when Burr was running for the governorship of New York, statesman Alexander Hamilton made some nasty remarks about his character. Burr promptly challenged Hamilton to a duel and killed him. It was clearly advisable for Burr to get away from the area, but he was again short of money. And so he obtained what he needed from Astor and gave some more of his land.

At just about the same time Astor took over a large farm that had belonged to a debt-ridden whisky distiller, named Eden. It was far above city limits and most people would not have thought it worth having. The Eden farm lay on what was to become Broadway from Forty-second to Forty-sixth Street. Fifty years after Astor's death, this land was to be worth twenty million dollars to his heirs.

On another occasion Astor heard a piece of gossip that he thought might be worth a fortune to him. A huge tract of valuable land had been confiscated from Roger and Mary Morris during the American Revolution because they were Tories. Astor learned that the land would have to be returned to the Morris children after the death of the parents. This was not generally known, and seven hundred families had bought farms on this property from the government. Mrs. Morris was still alive, but Astor, always a man to look ahead, went to the children and offered them a hundred thousand dollars for the land. It would then go to Astor when she died. After old Mrs. Morris' death at ninety-six, Astor calmly told the seven hundred families to get off his land. These farmers had improved the area and had built houses, barns, and cottages themselves. Nonetheless, John insisted that they were trespassing and that he had the right to take over their homes without paying them a penny. The government could not stand by and see such injustice and so Astor was given $520,000 in New York stocks in return for the land. Although the profit amounted to more than 500 per cent, Astor would have preferred to hold the real estate.

He kept a careful eye on the steady growth of New York. On the first of May Astor would go down to City Hall Park to see what was going on. This was the annual moving day in New York, and it was the custom for people carrying all their possessions to gather in the Park to wait for a house. No one knew where they came from or where they lived before. Perhaps relatives had sheltered some of them; others may have settled in huts as "squatters" on the swamplands and forests around the city. Every year at this time they appeared by the thousands. While trying to find homes for them, the city officials would lodge them in the jail. If a house was even half-finished, people would move into it. Officials reported that there was not a vacant house in the city. And yet in a single year 1,969 buildings had gone up.

Leaving the Park, Astor would walk slowly through the city, his squarely built body grown fat and flabby. It was still not easy walking, but now one of the hazards was that of falling into the excavation for a new house. Compared to the city of his youth, however, there were many cobblestone-paved streets. Canal Street had been laid out and went far beyond its start on the rolling fields given the city in the 1790's by John Jay. Bloomingdale Road (Broadway) was stretching northward through what had been woods only a short time before —nicely cutting through several pieces of Astor property and increasing their value considerably. The Bowery Road led out of the city to distant Harlem. New York was no longer a small town. The population had grown from 33,000 in 1790 to 96,000 in 1810 to 124,000 in 1820. Houses went up as fast as builders could work, and stores, banks, and warehouses to serve the people's needs were founded one after the other.

Today it seems obvious that this was only the beginning. But at the time no one believed the city could possibly get any bigger. There were farms and country estates in what is now the East Seventies. No one could possibly live there and commute to work in the city.

Astor did not agree. He had seen what furs and international trade—both of which he dominated—had done to stimulate the growth of New York as a business center. Boats were by this time going regularly from New York to England, France, and the southern ports of Savannah, Charleston, and New Orleans. In 1820 John Jacob fully expected New York to become what it is today. Using the money he was earning in furs and the China trade, he was able to buy land and make history work for him. During his lifetime he spent about two million dollars on real estate.

He was shrewd enough to realize that the way a piece of land looks today gives no hint of the way it will look tomorrow. A cabbage farm might someday be in the center of a fashionable neighborhood or business district. With this in mind, Astor tried to get land that looked worthless and was low in price. He bought dozens of lots on lower Broadway for two and three hundred dollars.

Astor never spent a penny on the property afterward;

he did not need to. Instead, he would rent the land and give the tenant a long-term lease, usually for twenty-one years. If the tenant wished to build a house on the land —and he almost always did—he could do so at his own expense. When the lease ran out, Astor had the right to buy the house, but he often preferred to renew the lease at a rent far higher than the old one. After all, the property was much more valuable with a building on it. Eventually John would rent only to someone who would agree to build a house on the land. He was a strict landlord. It was never wise to be late in paying the rent. Astor knew what was owing him on any given day—at any given hour, whispered some of his tenants.

An international trader as well as a real-estate investor, John Jacob wanted the rights to water-front property. When New York's port facilities became inadequate, and he never doubted that they would, he could build docks and charge for their use. The city, he was also sure, would be obliging enough to extend his property by filling in the river where it was shallow. In this way he would have some lots that had not even existed before. City officials were extremely generous in giving Astor water-front rights for the smallest possible sums. This was an era when money could buy power easily. A popular story of the time has a young man being offered a political job: "It's worth six hundred dollars a year—besides stealings." In order to gain power, Astor did not need to be a politician. He just needed to control politicians—and he did. Which party? It did not matter. If a man was useful, he was a friend.

Although Astor spent most of his time making money, he was, nonetheless, devoted to his family. The tragedy of his life was the condition of his eldest son. He hired a doctor-companion to stay with John Jacob II every moment. Whenever John became overexcited, the doctor would quiet him: "Astor, be a man." For a time he was confined to an institution, and eventually his father built a house for him surrounded by a high fence to conceal him from the curious.

John Jacob I found his greatest consolation in the company of his youngest and favorite daughter, Eliza. Even today the incredible sweetness of her face lights up the faded portrait of her that remains. Her eyes are glowing, her mouth so gentle that it is impossible to imagine her saying an unkind word. She often accompanied her father on his business trips to Canada, the Great Lakes region, or Europe. He hated to travel alone and his wife would not dream of journeying farther than Albany.

On one of the trips he performed the fatherly duty of arranging a marriage for Eliza with Count Vincent von Rumpff, minister of the German Free Cities. Gossips said that she was really in love with a Vermont dentist, Eleazar Parmly, but that her father had wanted a grander marriage for her. He had whisked her off to Paris and forced her to marry Von Rumpff. In the meantime, her mother had tried to foil John Jacob and to help the young sweethearts. She had sent for Parmly, had given him a thousand dollars to pay his expenses, and told him to leave for Europe and save Eliza. Alas, he had arrived too late! But the facts do not back up this romantic story. The panting young man arrived in Paris not a few days, weeks, or months too late to seize his beloved in his arms, but two whole years after her marriage.

The one undeniably true fact is that John Jacob was delighted with his new son-in-law. Count von Rumpff was able to have his father-in-law, who was after all a butcher's son, presented at the royal courts of Europe. As for Eliza, was she happy? If not, she never said so. She became very religious and established Sunday schools for children. Her father was desolate when she died, childless, at the age of thirty-seven in 1838.

He had by then lost his wife, Sarah, his eldest daughter, Magdalen, and his brother, butcher Henry. Unable to live alone, Astor took Magdalen's son, Charles Astor Bristed, into his home. For the most part, though, he buried his grief in his business.

"The man who makes it the habit of his life to go to bed at nine o'clock usually gets rich," he advised his quiet son, William. "Of course, going to bed does not make him rich—I merely mean that such a man will in all probability be up early in the morning and do a big day's work . . . it's all a matter of habit, and good habits in America make any man rich."

As he grew older, he became sentimental about the past. The skin of an otter was hung on the wall of his house. His piercing eyes would soften as he looked at the fine fur, and every so often he would stroke it gently. "How soft and beautiful it is!" he would mur-

mur. To him the otter was a symbol of the business that had laid the foundation for his immense fortune. He never forgot that without furs, there would have been no real estate.

John Jacob Astor became a millionaire by 1830 and a multimillionaire soon afterward. The great depression of that decade, the Panic of 1837, made most people desperately poor. Astor only grew richer out of the misfortunes of others.

"Two hundred and sixty houses have already failed, and no one knows when it is to end," wrote Captain Frederick Marryat, a British novelist, who visited New York at that time. "Had I not been aware of the cause, I should have imagined that the plague was raging. Not a smile on one countenance."

That last sentence cannot be completely true. Astor at least had cause to smile. As one of the few men in New York with ready cash, he was able to buy property all over the city. Desperate landowners were willing to sell at any price. By the time the Panic was over, Astor was so rich that he could hardly remember another way of life.

"A man who has a million dollars is as well off as if he were rich," he consoled a less fortunate friend.

Still, the Panic did do him some harm. It gave him New York, but took away his chance of owning the West. During the 1820's and early 1830's he had bought a lot of property around St. Louis, as well as territory in Wisconsin, Ohio, and Illinois. Suddenly he had another of his big ideas: he would found a city in Wisconsin that would bear the proud name of "Astor."

But Wisconsin was not New York and he had trouble finding people willing to live there and buy building lots from him. The Panic of 1837, so helpful in New York, finished off his hopes in Wisconsin. Most men were too short of money to gamble on the city of Astor, which in time became a part of Green Bay.

Astor's disappointment was considerably lessened by the success he was meeting in all other areas. Unquestioned ruler of Manhattan real estate, at the age of seventy he decided to go into a new business, that of hotel owner.

When planning the building of the Park Hotel (soon renamed Astor House), he went to dinner with a friend at another new hotel.

"This man will never succeed," said Astor.

"Why not?"

"Don't you see what large lumps of sugar he puts in the bowl?"

Despite this stingy attitude, John Jacob was determined to make his the finest hotel in the world. He set out to buy a whole block as a site, but one homeowner, Coster, held out until Astor offered sixty thousand dollars, nearly twice the value of the house and land. Even then he would not move out. The workers came and began wrecking the buildings on the block until only the Coster house was left. The men asked Astor what to do.

"Just start tearing down the house anyhow," he said,

"and—by the way—you might begin by taking away the steps."

Once this snag was out of the way the hotel went up, six stories high and with three hundred bedrooms. Astor felt that ten bathrooms would be more than enough, but was talked into seventeen. The daily rate for the rooms was set at the incredibly high rate of two dollars a day, including meals. Guests were served stewed kidneys in champagne sauce, corned leg of pork, roast loin of veal, boiled chicken, and a perfect soft vanilla custard.

From the day it was opened in 1836 the Astor House became a center for politicians and visiting celebrities. Abraham Lincoln, Henry Clay, Jefferson Davis, Edgar Allan Poe, and the Prince of Wales (later Edward VII) were just a few who stayed there over the years. The foreigners were dismayed by their view of New York. Novelist Charles Dickens stood on the steps before the main entrance and shuddered at the sight of pigs gobbling up the garbage.

When Davy Crockett was there, he was amazed to hear how much Astor had spent on the hotel. Assuming that the money came out of the fur business, he exclaimed: "Lord help the poor b'ars and beavers! They must be used to being skun by now."

Astor's fellow Americans tried to guess the exact amount of his wealth. The *New York Sun* named him the richest man in America, with a fortune of twenty million dollars.

Still, for all his wealth, waste continued to anger him.

John Jacob Astor

"He would never fail to reprove me for taking more butter on my plate than I could eat," recalled his grandson, Charles Astor Bristed.

And he went into a rage when another grandson's wife drew near to the fire wrapped in her furs, because heat ruins the valuable skins.

Astor was never generous with his money, always conscious of how hard he had worked to earn it. A minister called on him one day, seeking a contribution for a worthy cause. "You are indeed fortunate to have such a great fortune. It increases your ability to do good."

"Oh, the disposition to do good does not always increase with the means," replied Astor coolly.

John Jacob's one great charity was the Astor Library, which was to be the basis of the New York Public Library. The money for this was wheedled out of him with dogged persistence by Joseph Green Cogswell, a merchant who had once been a schoolteacher. Burning with enthusiasm, Cogswell could hardly wait to get to work, while Astor was in no hurry at all. Cogswell came to live with Astor and read aloud to him at night as his eyes were failing. They often discussed immortality, which had become a favorite topic of conversation. The subject of the library was much less appealing. At last Cogswell threatened to leave. Faced with the loss of his valued companion, John Jacob gave up, and Cogswell began to buy books. In Astor's will the library was put down for four hundred thousand dollars.

In his last years his health gave way. Usually at twilight he would painfully make his way out to the terrace of his home, supported by two servants, and watch the night boat going down the East River. But the time came when even this was too much for him. As he could not exercise, his doctor ordered that he be tossed in a blanket to improve the circulation of his blood.

Despite the failing body, Astor's mind remained clear. Those about him insisted that he still knew to the penny what rent was owing on each piece of property. As a result, people began to whisper a story about him that may, or may not, be true. His agent came to report on the rent collections and found John Jacob being tossed in his blanket. Nonetheless, Astor immediately remembered an aged lady who was late in paying her rent.

"Has she paid yet?" he gasped.

"She can't," replied the agent. "She simply doesn't have the money."

"She must pay!"

The agent went to Astor's son and asked him what to do. William Backhouse calmly counted out the money for the poor woman's rent and told the agent to bring the receipt to his father.

John Jacob was elated. "I knew you could get it, if you only went about it in the right way."

Death finally took Astor on March 29, 1848, when he was eighty-five years old. Most of the newspapers praised him to the skies. Not so the *New York Herald*, which called him "a self-invented money-making machine."

But even when Astor was alive, there had been no agreement as to his character. The making of a fortune had been his ambition and in fulfilling it he created a legend. Brilliant, bold, daring, vigorous, possessed of financial genius . . . this is how he was viewed by most of the people of his time. Cold, calculating, crafty, unscrupulous, unprincipled, grasping . . . this is the image held by those who competed with him in the fur trade, export-import, or real estate. Warm, loving, sentimental, charming, vital, magnetic . . . this is how he was known to his friends and family. Crude, vulgar, illmannered . . . this is the opinion held by members of society of his day. Each of these images is true; the man was all of these things—and more. Even putting them all together does not give a complete picture of the complex, contradictory nature of John Jacob Astor, who rose out of poverty to become the richest man in America and to found one of the country's great dynasties.

Astor's personality was so forceful that not only his money, but also his wishes were passed on to his children and grandchildren. For many generations they lived as if his hands were directing them.

2

William Backhouse Astor and the City of New York

HE GREW UP in the shadow of his father, a quiet boy, an obedient boy. There are no legends about William Backhouse Astor. He did not make a fortune by trading furs to Indians in the wilderness, or send an expedition to Astoria, or trick a President into letting his ship go through a blockade. It fell to him to keep the books and manage the details of his father's business.

Most people envied the son of John Jacob Astor for the wealth that was handed to him. His father had earned a quarter of a million dollars by the time William was eight. But one of William's few close friends said of him: "He sat in his office as if it were a prison to which his father had condemned him for life."

William never rebelled, or even tried to rebel; he was prepared to fill the role of heir from early childhood. Although different in almost every way from his dynamic father, his character was formed by the loving, overpowering nature of John Jacob. The only time in his life when he was free of his father was during the years when he attended the University of Göttingen in Germany. Although the Astors are closely connected with the growth of America, they remained German in a number of ways for many years. John spoke German to his children all his life and William was to do the same with his.

Possessing an earnest and scholarly mind, William applied himself seriously to his studies. His vacations were spent in Europe, because it was obviously impossible to return to distant America with only a month or two of free time. And so he was in Europe when the War of 1812 broke out. Europe was not at peace either, with Napoleon waging war. John Jacob became frantic with worry.

"William is no more!" he exclaimed in a moment of despair.

When he learned that William was alive, Astor swung into action. He wanted his boy safe at home. True, New York harbor was blockaded and no ships were being allowed to get through, but rules were something that Astor felt applied to other people. He had broken blockades before, and he could do it again. This time he found French General Jean Victor Moreau, who was burning with desire to fight against Napoleon. How could he return to Europe? On Astor's ship, the *Hannibal,* of course. As John Jacob could not resist the pleasure (and profit) of getting furs out of blockaded

New York right from under the noses of the British enemy, the ship left the harbor carrying both the general and a valuable cargo of furs. On the way back William was a somewhat unwilling passenger, displeased at having been forced to cut short his European adventure.

After the war, John Jacob, showing his customary indulgence where his family was concerned, sent William back with permission to spend whatever he wanted. William kept a record of all travel expenses, noting down every cup of coffee. It turned out that he was like his father when it came to the careful use of money.

"He spent only ten thousand dollars!" John could not get over it. "I thought he would certainly spend fifty thousand dollars."

Perhaps such a mature young man was already capable of taking his place in his father's office. William accepted the offer without question and set about helping his father in the demanding task of increasing the wealth that was someday to be his. Perhaps, as has been said, he was a prisoner in the office, but prisoners sometimes grow fond of their cells. If William was unhappy there, he was probably not happy anywhere else. But then, no one, even in his own time, knew very much about William's dreams and ambitions. John Jacob's personality was so vivid that still today it leaps from the pages of old documents and letters. In contrast, records tell very little about William as a man. At least old pictures can tell us what he looked like. An old miniature treasured by a surviving great-granddaughter shows the surprising fact that he was a handsome boy with fresh coloring and soft, wavy brown hair. The years were not kind to his looks, however, and by the time he reached manhood, his features had taken on a heavy Germanic cast.

"William was the richest and least attractive young man of his time," said an acquaintance with brutal frankness.

He had not been lucky enough to escape the Astor nose or the small eyes. Although he was tall and powerfully built, he had the unfortunate habit of slouching. Completely lacking vitality, he was shy and sluggish, showing so little emotion that he was generally believed to be a cold man.

None of this kept him from being the most eligible bachelor in America. Society was busy guessing what lucky girl would get him, which really meant, of course, who John Jacob would decide was a suitable bride. William met the girl who was to win him on one of the rare occasions when his father let him go to Albany to discuss real-estate legislation with Judge Ambrose Spencer. The Judge's house guest that day happened to be Margaret Rebecca Armstrong, a rather plain eighteen-year-old with thin, tight lips that made her seem prim. William hardly noticed that, though, being struck by the beauty of her complexion which had the soft, lovely coloring of a fresh peach. His father was equally struck by her background. Her grandfather, General John A. Armstrong, a fighter in the French and Indian War, so distinguished himself as a brigadier general in the Revolution that the state of Pennsylvania made a medal in his honor. Her father, General John A. Armstrong II, had been a notable military leader in the Revolution and War of 1812, and had later become Secretary of the State of Pennsylvania, U.S. Senator, U.S. Minister to France and to Spain, and Secretary of War.

Margaret was a deeply religious girl, which appealed to William, as his mother had trained him to read the Bible regularly, marking the passages that meant the most to him. On Sundays he attended church both morning and afternoon.

After arranging this most suitable marriage, John Jacob looked for a home that would be good enough for the favored young couple. Rich people were living in what is now the business district. Wellborn New Yorkers took their Sunday strolls on a broad promenade near the river. Grownups tried to stay away from the area on Saturday, as boys played ball and there was always danger of being hit. Few cared to go driving, for dust rose from the partly paved streets to swirl in great clouds about the heads of anyone in the carriage. The house selected by Astor was on Broadway and White Street, an elegant block with painted brick houses and a flagstone sidewalk kept scrupulously clean by servants. All the water used for drinking, bathing, and cleaning was carried by the servants from a pump on the corner. Still, this was better than collecting rain water as poorer people had to do throughout much of the nineteenth century. Milk was delivered to the door by men carrying large tin cans suspended from a yoke across their shoulders.

Once settled in his new home with his wife, shy William relaxed enough to give her a pet name—"Peachy," because of her soft, glowing skin. This is one of the few touches of human sentiment to be found about him in the family records.

William set his life into a pattern and followed it until four days before his death at the age of eighty-three. He got up early and wrote letters before eating breakfast. This meal was served to him at nine o'clock. Then he walked to the office, arriving at ten. At the end of his day's work, he walked home. Sometimes he strolled through the blocks where the shops were located. Each store listed the things it had to sell on placards attached to wooden pillars that stood on the edge of the pavements. In summer he was grateful for the awnings that stretched from the stores to the street. It was still necessary to walk carefully on the pitted roads. The walk was partly for economy, as William did not believe in wasting a penny. He spent very little on his clothes—too little, some members of his family complained. As a result, he often looked sloppy, particularly as despite all the walking, he got fat while still young.

Margaret presented him with three daughters and three sons, and William played favorites. He adored his firstborn, Emily, and favored his eldest son, John Jacob III, as heir apparent, while rather ignoring the rest.

Most of his energies went into helping his father in business. No piece of work was too small for him. He checked and rechecked every expenditure. Was it really necessary? Could the job be done more cheaply? He inspected furs, investigated tenants, kept track of every dollar owing.

"William was really no better than a head clerk—a very good clerk, and a trusted one—but an underling, nonetheless," commented one of his friends long afterward.

This was even true of the American Fur Company in which his father had given him the title of president. All that he had was the title, however; John was still in charge. William was a religious man and did not approve of selling liquor to the Indians. He even tried to do something about it and appealed to other fur traders to join in an agreement to stop. But his well-meaning effort fell through, possibly because John Jacob was not behind it. John believed that religion had no place in business, and gradually William came to agree with him.

In his father's position, William would never have made the fortune in the first place. Once it was made, he succeeded in doubling it. "Take care of what you have. That is what makes the money grow." This was the policy that ruled William's life.

He was helped, of course, by the growth of New York. William had inherited his father's vision of a great New York. As he always followed John's advice, he decided to buy some land himself. His father had told him that the city was expanding northward, and so one day in 1826 William, his nervousness hidden by his unemotional manner, agreed to pay the Thompson family twenty-five thousand dollars for a huge plot of rather poor farmland. John Jacob was right; the Thompson farm was on what is now Thirty-second to Thirty-fourth Streets on Fifth and Madison Avenues. The Empire State Building stands on just one corner of it. Fifteen years later William sold a single lot—no Astor cared to sell more—at auction for twelve hundred dollars.

Although he had to wait until he was middle-aged to inherit his father's millions, William became a millionaire himself long before that. Some of his money was earned through opportunities thrown his way by John Jacob; the rest came from his uncle Henry, who selected William as his heir.

The possession of the butcher's money sent William in search of a new address. The part of the city where he lived had become overcrowded, and streets only a few blocks away were repulsive. Sanitary conditions in early nineteenth century America were unbelievably bad. The water that was still being sold to people far from the pumps was often contaminated. Epidemics of cholera, dysentery, and yellow fever swept through the area again and again. Fear spread among the rich homeowners; they were not far enough away from the poor to be safe. Sunday strollers no longer dared to walk along the river front. Everyone who could afford to move did so, knowing no other way to escape the disease. Many built houses on the rolling fields of Greenwich Village. A potter's field where the poor had been buried was filled in to form Washington Square.

William asked his father what to do, and as it turned out, John just happened to own the perfect piece of property on Lafayette Place. William built his mansion there of red brick, and another house was built for his sister, Dorothea Langdon, and her family on the corner lot at Art Street, soon to be renamed Astor Place. Their father considered taking that one for himself, but he was superstitious and believed that corner lots were unlucky for him. On Sundays New Yorkers used to drive down Lafayette Place to stare at the mansions and wait for the Astors to come out as if they were movie or television stars.

Even Lafayette Place was not considered safe from epidemics in the summer. And so it was customary for well-to-do families to leave the city. For this purpose, John Jacob had given William and Margaret the wedding present that she wanted above all else—her family home to use as a country estate. Margaret, who loved romantic poetry, renamed it "Rokeby" after a poem by Sir Walter Scott. Still in the possession of John Jacob's descendants, Rokeby is filled with the pictures, papers, books, and furnishings of generations of Astors. Even today it remains magnificent in its very shabbiness. Its original upholstery is threadbare now and there are only remnants of the delicate, flowered wallpaper that was put up in the early years of the nineteenth century.

Big as it was, the house did not seem large enough to William, as his father-in-law and a bachelor brother-in-law, Kosciusko Armstrong, continued to live with him. To house these relatives as well as his own family, William added an entire wing.

Although practical in running his business, William

was not efficient when it came to his own home, and he seldom consulted his wife about anything. Although the dining room was on the ground floor of the original house, for example, William had an enormous kitchen placed on the second floor of the new wing. This meant that food had to be carried from the stove all the way across a long pantry and then sent down by dumbwaiter. Waited on by servants, William may never have noticed how awkward it was.

By the time he reached the plans for what was to be his favorite room, a huge, eight-sided library, he had begun to worry about the amount of money he was spending. Being a millionaire did not make him careless. He decided to save a few dollars by having the plaster ceiling painted to look like wood. A scholarly man, William was in later years often found sitting by the fireplace in the library. His reading, however, according to his family, was usually limited to German encyclopedias and dictionaries, of which he had a large collection.

One shelf, of gardening books, was Margaret's. Gardening was her delight, and even in the city, she kept the windows of her sitting room filled with plants. She was pleased by William's decision to keep on running part of the estate as a farm.

Recognizing her love of flowers, William once gave her a choice: "Should I give you money to establish an orphanage, Peachy, or to build a greenhouse for flowers?"

Margaret thought it over. "I would dearly love to

have a greenhouse," she replied. "But as I am a good Christian woman, I know that the orphanage should come first."

"That is the right answer," returned William. "You shall have both."

Whether at Rokeby or Lafayette Street, William's thoughts were centered on real estate. Obeying his father, he hardly ever sold a foot of it, preferring to rent the land. When he first joined the business, the yearly rent for a single lot was between $50.00 and $87.50. But as New York grew, each piece of property became more valuable.

William noted that in 1825 alone, five hundred new business firms opened up, along with twelve banks and ten insurance companies. The building of three thousand houses got underway. The postoffice had to take on six clerks to handle the mail being sent by those able to afford 12½ cents postage to Philadelphia, 18¾ cents to Boston, and 25 cents to New Orleans. Back in 1812 when the idea of street lights had first been presented, it was dismissed as absurd and extravagant. By 1825, however, gas lights were installed on a few of the streets, and within ten years many parts of the city were lighted at night. Robert Fulton's invention, the steamboat, served to bring Brooklyn and Jersey City within comparatively easy reach. Steam ferries made the journey back and forth. There was another ferry to take people across the East River, but it did not altogether replace rowboats anchored at the foot of Wall Street. An oarsman would take a passenger across for ten cents a trip.

In 1832 the New York and Harlem Railroad Company ran horsecars between Prince and Fourteenth streets, giving the city its first public-street transportation. Only two years later steam trolley cars took passengers seventy blocks farther uptown.

Thirteen hundred sailing ships entered New York harbor each year, bringing people and cargoes from all over the world. In the month of May, 1837, fifty-seven hundred immigrants entered the country. The housing shortage, severe when Astor had first watched the homeless gathering in City Hall Park, had become steadily worse.

Fires often destroyed the houses that had been built. One of the worst, in 1835, leveled thousands of buildings to the ground, seven hundred in what is now the financial district. Any fire was almost impossible to check in a large city with no running water and only volunteer firemen. Just one man was posted atop the City Hall to spot fires, sound the alarm, and then send the volunteers to the blaze by waving a lantern in the right direction. A fire engine would eventually be dragged to the scene by a crew of twenty-six men and would pump water from either the Hudson or East River. It was clear that a new source of water was needed to fight fires, as well as to drink and use for washing. The Croton Reservoir and Aqueduct was built north of New York to run into a city reservoir located on Forty-second Street where the New York Public Library stands today.

By this time in the early 1840's the Astors were able

to get one hundred-and-seventy-five dollars a year rent for a single lot. If a house was on the land, the rent varied from six hundred to fourteen hundred dollars, depending on size and location. Everyone complained about the high cost of housing, recalling that in the 1820's, three hundred dollars a year was a rent a rich man would pay for a good house on a good block. Everyone complained, except the Astors, who grew richer and richer.

William had been the most eligible bachelor of his day, and his children were the most sought-after marriage partners of theirs. Sam Ward, Jr., son of a noted banker and a descendant of two former governors of Rhode Island, set his sights high, on William's eldest daughter. Emily was as unlike an Astor as it was possible for a child of this family to be. Her father's long face and stodgy manner did not dampen her high spirits and she went through life with a smile. With reddish-gold hair, sapphire-blue eyes, and the pleasingly plump figure that was considered ideal at that time, she was her parents' joy and her grandfather's pet. He would listen for hours to her beautiful soprano voice.

Shrewd Sam quickly realized that he had to win not only the girl and her father, but also her forceful grandfather. "He was full of jokes for the old man," one of his friends recalled. "He once brought a ventriloquist to the estate."

Sam was so successful at pleasing Astor that the young couple received a house on Bond Street as a wedding gift. But the marriage of Emily and Sam was as short as it was happy. She died of fever after childbirth in 1841 when she was just twenty-two years old. The family never fully recovered from her loss.

"Mother became a different woman," Margaret's surviving children said sadly. "From a genial person, she changed into a stern, quiet one. She could never bring herself to mention Emily's name again."

Handsome, dashing Sam had loved Emily, but he was not the type to mourn for long, and he was married again soon afterward. Sam's sister, Louisa, was visiting at Rokeby when news of the second marriage arrived. For once William lost his calm and flew into a rage all the more terrifying because it was so unusual. "Order the carriage for Miss Ward at once!" he shouted.

John Jacob was just as furious as was William, and demanded that Emily's small daughter, Margaret "Maddie" Astor Ward, be sent to the Astors. Although the arrangements for this were as usual made by the old man, it was the William B. Astors who took the child into their home.

Three years after Emily's tragic death, her younger sister, Laura, an exceedingly plain girl, married Franklin Hughes Delano. A female relative has remembered him as "one of the best-looking men of his day." At the wedding at Rokeby this girl was so overcome that she backed into the French windows and nearly fell out onto the lawn. Both John Jacob and William were delighted with this match and presented the couple with a fortune. The one great regret of the Delanos was that they had no children to share their wealth. There was a niece, however, Sara Delano, who was to become the mother of Franklin Delano Roosevelt. When he was born, Sara wanted to name him Warren. Her family talked her into naming the child after "Uncle Frank who was so good to us all."

The youngest of William's daughters, Alida, was married to John Carey, Jr., an Englishman. The unkind gossip of the time said that he had come here to marry an American girl with a fortune. If so, Carey picked the right one. Alida brought him two hundred thousand dollars in cash and another hundred thousand in real estate.

During all these years William's sister, Dorothea Langdon, lived right next door to him, growing steadily fatter. Only one of her eight children inherited the rebellious nature that had prompted her own elopement years earlier. This girl, Louisa, while out for a drive with her sister Eliza, remarked innocently that she needed to buy something at Peiser's dry goods store. "I'll just be a minute," she told her sister. "You wait for me in the carriage."

Eliza waited, but her sister did not come back. Finally she went into the store where the clerk informed her that Louisa had come in, walked through the shop and out the back door. There was nothing to be done, so Eliza went home to lunch.

Just as the pudding was being served, the message arrived: Louisa had eloped with Oliver DeLancey Kane. History promptly repeated itself. Her father, Colonel Langdon, was not softened by remembering how he had been cut off by John Jacob Astor. Refusing to listen to the pleas of his tender-hearted wife, he announced that he was washing his hands of the wild young pair. Her uncle William cut Louisa out of his will, but relented in time to put her back in.

Wills were taken very seriously by this family. John Jacob's will had been worked and reworked and changed again until he was satisfied that the fortune would last not only through William's day, but would be there for William's sons, John Jacob III and William Backhouse, Jr., and for their sons in turn.

William was fifty-six years old on that March day in 1848 when his father died. His entire life had been a preparation for this event. Head of the house at last, William showed a side of his nature that no one had even thought existed. He had been considered a stingy man, a penny pincher. Once all the pennies were his, however, he was more generous than his father had been. He discovered that his father's former secretary, Fitz-Greene Halleck, had been left two hundred dollars a year. Upon questioning the man, it turned out that Halleck had once remarked to his employer: "Of what use is all this money to you, Mr. Astor? I would be content to live on a couple of hundred a year for the rest of my life, if I was only sure of it."

Halleck had been joking, but John Jacob, who sometimes had a rather cruel sense of humor, had left Halleck exactly that amount. William had no sense of humor at all; he could not see the joke. His logical mind simply told him that it was unfair, and he raised the sum to fifteen hundred dollars.

"William B. Astor is the best man in the United States to have charge of a colossal fortune," reported a writer of the period.

Then William took his father's single great charity, the Astor Library, in hand and sent Cogswell off to Europe to buy books. He also added some money to complete the building. With his push behind it, the Astor Library opened in 1854 holding more than eighty thousand books. These were not to be taken out; the Library was to be a place to do research only. No one thought of starting a free public lending library. In New York most people well-educated enough to read for pleasure—and they were a minority—bought their own books or joined a private library for a fee.

It did not take schoolboys long to discover the Astor Library. "Youngsters out of school read trashy books by Sir Walter Scott, Charles Dickens, and James Fenimore Cooper," Cogswell declared sadly. He consoled himself with the thought that "even this is better than spinning street yarns."

One day Cogswell went into the library and discovered schoolboys copying English versions of the Latin and Greek works they were supposed to translate for homework. The old scholar was horrified and insisted that the minimum age for use of the Library immediately be raised from fourteen to sixteen. After all, no mature sixteen-year-old could stoop so low as to copy someone else's work.

In only a year it became clear that the library needed to be enlarged, and so William contributed more land and money.

Along with the library and the complete charge of the business, William inherited the problem of his insane brother, John Jacob Astor II. William investigated the arrangements which his father had made. Shocked to discover that his brother's physician-companion was being paid five thousand dollars a year, he fired the doctor and hired a lower-priced guardian instead. As soon as John Jacob II realized that the doctor was gone, he flew into a rage. A big, powerful man, he broke windows and threw furniture about. When he had exhausted himself, he lay on the bed and cried. William was not a cruel man. Upon discovering how deeply his brother felt, he asked the doctor to return.

"I'm not coming back," replied the physician. "I'm a free man for the first time in years."

When William offered to raise his salary to ten thousand dollars, he agreed to go back. It would be nice to think that he might have cared a little about John Jacob II whose face looks out of the only portrait painted of him with an expression of intolerable sadness. All his father's money had not saved him from the tortures of his own mind.

William's feelings about his brother were no doubt related to a problem much closer to his heart. In addition to John Jacob III and William Backhouse, Jr., there was another son, Henry, who was hardly known outside of the immediate family. The parents did not approve of his marriage to Malvina Dinehart, whose father had worked as a gardener for the Astors. They were also distressed by his strange behavior.

Henry built a house with its own private race track and a room paved with silver dollars. Six feet tall and muscular, with a flaming red beard, he was terrifying when he flew into one of his violent rages. In other moods, he would put on a surplice and preach sermons, striking a bell with a crowbar to emphasize his points. His brothers managed his estate for him and did such a good job that when Henry died at the age of eighty-eight, his property was sold at a huge real-estate auction for $5,159,075. It was a mere nothing, though, compared to the immense wealth gathered for his brothers by their father.

A catch phrase is often attached to the names of well-known people. John Jacob I was the "richest man in America"; William Backhouse became the "landlord of New York." Real estate was his passion. He let someone else manage the Astor House hotel—checking all expenses and repairs, naturally—and he did not try to run any of the companies in which he owned stock. Land was another matter. There was not a rock on the ground or a brick on a wall that was unimportant to him. He watched over these possessions from the office of the Astor Estate.

The Astor Estate sounds important, but the office was very simple. There were only two rooms. In the first of these, one or two clerks were checking figures and young John Jacob III was hard at work on the books. Like his father before him, he was being trained in the business. The second room, which was plainly furnished, was William's office. The door was not shut. Anyone could go in to see him; not many dared.

"I would walk into his office and he would look up without speaking," remarked a businessman of the period. "He would look at me, but ask no questions. It was up to me to tell him what I was there for. And it was clear that he would like me to do so in as few words as possible. He would answer as if each word were worth a dollar."

Every dollar went into buying more real estate. The value of his property increased constantly, partly as a result of events taking place far from New York. One of the most important of these began in the summer of 1845 when the farmers in Ireland looked over their fields and saw brown spots on the leaves of their potato plants. Soon the potatoes began to rot. Potatoes were Ireland's only crop and more than a third of the Irish ate nothing else. As a result, the potato blight brought starvation on a scale that has seldom been equaled in all history. During the six years of famine, nearly two million Irish left their country forever. A million-and-a-half made their way to the United States, arriving starving, sick, and penniless. During those same years, political unrest drove thousands of Germans to this country, too. The majority of these immigrants settled in New York. By 1850 nearly half the city's population had been born abroad.

Every one of these immigrants had to find a place to

live. One might think that these unfortunate people would have been too poor to pay the kind of rent that enriches a landlord, but there is a way of making money out of the poor. The system is to crowd people together miserably, charging each one the largest amount he can possibly afford. Anyone able to multiply can figure that ten families, each paying nine dollars-a-month rent for the single apartment they share are giving the landlord more money than he could get from one family paying fifty dollars.

What did a typical tenement, as these apartment houses came to be known, look like? The buildings themselves were, surprisingly enough, rather fancy on the outside, with carved stone entrances and arched door-ways. This does not mean that the slum blocks were attractive at first glance. The toilets were outside and each had to be used by so many people that it became repulsive. Until well into the 1860's pigs and hungry slum children competed for the rotting scraps of food in the garbage thrown into the gutters. The few street cleaners employed by the city seldom ventured into the poorer neighborhoods.

Inside the building was a layout that had been de-signed as if four families and no more would live on each floor of a tenement. Actually every apartment was shared by several families, despite the fact that only the living room deserved the name of "room," being twelve feet long by ten feet wide. The bedrooms were no larger than a clothes closet in a modern home. Sometimes a second house was fastened onto the rear wall of the first, so as to increase the number of people who could be housed on the same bit of land. Obviously, the second house cut down on the light and air.

"The very dogs and cats would, if unmolested, prefer the open street," the Reverend Peter Stryker declared from his pulpit in the Thirty-fourth Street Reformed Dutch Church, after a visit to the slums. "The . . . tenement houses . . . are a standing reproach against our rich men who ought, for the sake of humanity, to be using their surplus funds in erecting cheap and comfortable residences for the poor."

The thought never entered the minds of Astor and the other major landlords. The tenements were not put up by William Astor, or in later years by his sons. The Astors, and many other landowners, simply rented the land, and left it to a sublandlord to build and in turn rent a house. These sublandlords had to pay the Astors rent for the land, and then improve it, put up the building, and pay the taxes. They quickly saw that the best way for them to make a profit was not only to squeeze as many people as possible into each house and to charge high rents, but also to make no repairs at all. This last policy meant that the buildings would go downhill, with broken floors, crumbling plaster, and rickety stairs. But the sublandlords did not care, and Astor flatly refused to pay a penny for upkeep. The run-down tenements sometimes brought in even more money than the newer ones. The very poorest people would go to them, offering to pay rent for a tiny piece of a room. In time, some of the tenements were to sink so low that tramps paid three cents just to spend a night in the hallways, sheltered from the cold.

How could William Astor, eating off his gold plates, endure the knowledge of such misery? He did know that the tenements existed; he kept a careful eye on each piece of property. But he was able to blame the sublandlords for the conditions. They were greedy, he would say. The fact that he was as much to blame never even occurred to him. William had been brought up to think of money and property, not of people. His good impulses, such as his wish to stop selling whisky to the Indians, were stopped short by the father in whom he had absolute confidence. He was the son of a man who had considered it right to be good to his family and unscrupulous in his dealings with others. How much could he earn? That was the question he had been trained to ask. He saw the tenements not as a source of tragedy, but only as a source of income. William had never been poor and he did not understand it. He liked to remind people that his father had landed in America with nothing, and look what he had made of himself! Surely any hard-working young fellow could do the same. If a man was poor, it was because he was lazy. There was nothing pitiful about it. William walked through the city of New York as if he had blinkers on.

In another man such blindness would not have mattered, but William was in a position to change much of the city. Instead, he permitted the tenements to rise on one Astor lot after the other.

William kept right on buying. He purchased slum

property and also land far from where anyone was living. Some day, he thought, people might even venture to live near that new Central Park being laid out in the countryside north of Fifty-ninth Street. It might not happen for a long time, but William could wait. His possessions gradually extended from downtown to uptown, from East Side to West, on more avenues, streets, farms, and wooded areas than one could count.

City politicians were eager to help so powerful a landlord. By the middle of the nineteenth century they had learned that slum landlords were a candidate's best friends. The poor people living in the tenements could be rounded up and influenced or if necessary paid to vote on Election Day. Some of them had arrived in the United States so recently that they had not become citizens. The politicians repaid Astor and the other big real-estate owners by keeping their taxes very low.

There were few favors that Astor could not get from Democratic Mayor Fernando B. Wood and his corrupt city government. Wood meant to get rich in office and paid little attention to conditions in the city. The new, small police department could not cope with the large number of thefts. Violence was so common that one block was given the expressive and accurate name of "Murderers' Alley."

In 1856 when Wood wanted to run for re-election he met opposition from members of his own Democratic party who were sickened by his dishonesty. A report praising him was hastily drawn up. (His enemies insisted that he wrote it himself.) It was signed by some of the most prominent men in the city, among them William B. Astor. With such support, Wood was re-elected.

Within the next few years, conflict grew between the North and South, and Civil War clouds gathered. Mayor Wood favored the South and he suggested that New York become an independent city, rather than help the North. Abraham Lincoln, who was then running for the Presidency, remarked that this was hardly the time for the front door to detach itself and set up housekeeping. William Astor thought that Wood was going too far, but he was afraid that war might cause the value of his real estate to fall. His sons begged him to support Lincoln, but he never listened to them. And so he opposed Abraham Lincoln and the Republican party. A month after Lincoln's election, Senator John Jordan Crittenden of Kentucky sponsored a compromise designed to prevent civil war by amending the Constitution to allow slavery in some states and not in others. Astor seized on this as the perfect solution, and together with thirty other business leaders, held a mass meeting urging the acceptance of this amendment.

The firing on Fort Sumter in April, 1861, brought an end to hopes of compromise. To the relief of his sons, William promptly announced that he was a loyal citizen of the Union and would stand by it to the end.

William was pleasantly surprised by the effect of war on real estate. Rents rose to new high levels. By the time the Civil War was over, William's political affections had been won by the Republicans. He threw his support to Andrew Johnson and then to Ulysses S. Grant, who became a fast friend of the family.

On the other hand, William was infuriated by a wartime effort to raise money by means of an income tax. In 1865, with an income of $1,300,000, he was handed the largest tax bill of any individual in the United States. After the war William called in his lawyers and insisted that they get the income tax removed. They were so persuasive that the Supreme Court found the income tax to be unconstitutional.

By this time the Astor family had become prominent members of society and William tried to forget the humble origins of his family. John Jacob I had commissioned portraits of his parents in which they were shown as poor peasants selling fish, game, and flowers. Sold after John's death, the pictures were bought back into the family by William's niece, Eliza. Upon seeing them in her home, William asked for them. As he appeared even more somber than usual, she questioned why he wanted them. "To burn them," he replied coldly.

Although welcomed everywhere, there was little in social life that appealed to William. He found it painful to tear himself away from his work for any reason. Despite his European education, he went abroad only once with his wife. Traveling in solid comfort, they experienced but one night of excitement in Italy when the volcano Vesuvius threatened to erupt. The proprietor of their hotel awakened all the guests and asked them to move to a safer place. Everyone did so hurriedly, except for the Astors. William B. Astor was seen pacing up and down in front of the hotel, waiting for Margaret.

Upon being urged to make his wife hurry, William replied: "My wife is a general's daughter. She cannot be made to feel frightened."

For all that she was a general's daughter, Margaret was not really more adventurous than her husband. The world that mattered to her was the narrow, feminine one of home, children, her garden, the church, and the charities she sponsored.

"Mrs. Astor gave us our first gift—fifty dollars," said Reverend Charles Loring Brace, founder of the Children's Aid Society.

The Dutchess County orphanage, given her along with the greenhouse, housed and educated fourteen girls. Her largest single contribution, of a thousand dollars, went to the New York Women's Hospital, which also received a regular yearly donation of a hundred dollars. These figures are small in terms of her husband's one-million-dollars-plus-a-year income. Still, Margaret did as well as she could in a time when social consciousness on the part of the rich had not yet been awakened. A bowl of soup or a jar of jelly brought to a starving family was still considered suitable charity for a lady.

With all of society's gaiety available to her, this was her life. She died in 1872, fifty-four years after her marriage. The usually stolid, unemotional William was terribly upset by her death. The only thing that gave him pleasure was to have Emily's daughter, Maddie, read the Bible to him. Maddie had grown up to marry handsome John Winthrop Chanler, a politician. She bore him eleven children.

One of these children, Margaret Chanler, used to come into her great-grandfather's room to try to cheer him up. "If you will whistle the tune of 'St. Patrick's Day in the Morning,' I will jig it," she would say to him, but he would only answer sadly that he did not know the tune.

William died in 1875, having lived for eighty-three years. For a good number of them, he was the richest man in America, but the general public knew him only as a name. Still, if he was not an interesting personality of himself, he helped to make possible an interesting time. His influence on the New York that made his family wealthy was tremendous. Without him, the Astors would never have obtained such control over the real estate of the city or such power with politicians. His lack of understanding and imagination—for he was not an evil man—allowed the tenements to flourish. The "money-making machine" John Jacob Astor I had been accused of inventing was really his son rather than himself.

3

John Jacob Astor III—
Gentleman, Soldier, and Landlord

"HE HAD THE AIR of reserve and dignity, the bearing which marks a man to whom by nature, place and honor belong."

This description of John Jacob Astor III was made by the Reverend Morgan Dix, a prominent nineteenth-century clergyman.

John's confidence and natural air of superiority were encouraged by his father, who gave him favored-son treatment all his life. From the time they were boys, William completely ignored the fact that the younger son, William Backhouse, Jr., was brighter than his brother.

John went to college at Columbia where he "failed of distinction," according to a harsh report uncovered recently in an old issue of *Harper's Weekly*. (His brother, on the other hand, made an outstanding college record, graduating second in his class.) Nonetheless, the family determined to send John to Göttingen to continue his education in Astor style. They were still German enough to call him "Johann" among themselves.

Joseph Cogswell was asked to accompany him. It probably was not much fun for John to go abroad with an aging scholar, but he was not allowed to refuse. In the Astor family, the father's word was law. Young Astor and Cogswell spent two years at Göttingen. Cogswell was rewarded for his services with sixty thousand dollars for the library, and John came out well enough prepared for a year at Harvard Law School.

His father did not wish him to become a practising lawyer. The Astors employed the best lawyers of the day, but they thought it wise for a member of the family to have a smattering of knowledge about deeds and leases, water rights, and laws. John, therefore, followed his year at Harvard with another in a law office. By 1843, at the age of twenty-one, he was considered ready to meet the Astor fate in the real-estate office.

John Jacob III was the first of the Astors to be bored by the business that fascinated both his father and grandfather. He cut his working hours to a minimum, accompanied his father on the walk to the office each morning at nine, stopped at noon for lunch, and then worked again until three. It cannot be denied that John worked hard during these short hours. Despite his poor showing at Columbia, he followed his father's teaching very well. As the Astor fortune continued to grow, John decided that his short hours were somehow responsible.

In time, he was to advise others: "Work hard, but never work after dinner."

Strangers found young Astor rather frightening. He stood six feet tall in an era when many men were half a foot shorter, and he had a commanding presence as well. His light-gray eyes were keen and searching, his complexion ruddy, and he wore a flowing mustache and sideburns. The formality of his manners did not put others at their ease. His inborn feeling of superiority was of no help in finding subjects to talk about. He was comfortable with just a few good friends.

One of the only girls with whom John felt relaxed was Charlotte Augusta Gibbes, with whom he had grown up. Physically, Augusta—she seldom used her first name—was almost his exact opposite, being small, blonde, and frail. She was not beautiful, as her nose was too long, but she had great charm and everybody who met her was drawn to her.

"The better sort have been regaled by a good wedding . . . attended at the house of her father by all the fashionable people of the city." This entry appeared in a diary kept by Philip Hone, one-time mayor of New York, describing the wedding of Augusta and John Jacob III.

The match, as was true of most at that period, had been arranged by the two sets of parents. But those who knew the couple say the marriage was happy.

Although John Jacob III was to be a millionaire, Augusta was economical, conscious that he was dependent upon his father.

John Jacob Astor III

"As long as William Backhouse lived, Augusta and her husband practised extreme simplicity of household management," reported a curious neighbor. "Her dress was plain and so was her home."

John Jacob III applauded her economies. He kept track of the household expenses as if he would be sent to one of his father's tenements for spending too much.

In 1848 Augusta gave birth to the only child she was to have. He was named William Waldorf in an effort to combine his grandfather's name with his great-grandfather's place of birth. (The reason for the dropping of an "l" from Walldorf has never been satisfactorily explained.) John Jacob III was delighted to have an heir who would one day take over the Astor Estate.

The only part of the business that John Jacob really enjoyed was the buying of new property. He liked to keep a large sum of ready cash on hand. "You never know when you'll see a good buy," he told one of the clerks in the Estate office. "I want to be able to pick up a bargain on the spot."

William allowed his more daring son to do so, because he remembered his own brilliant youthful purchase of the highly profitable Thompson Farm. Even as a young man, John had grasped the sense of the family policy of buying undeveloped land outside the populated areas. He knew that when his father was a boy, sportsmen had gone duck and quail hunting in places where homes and factories now stood. A few hardy souls were daring to settle in suburban Harlem. Perhaps someday people would be living in the wilds of what was known simply as the "Annexed District."

That rural area had been granted to Colonel Lewis Morris in 1676 by England's King Charles II, but his descendants did not prosper and the Morris holdings shrank acre by acre. On a winter's day in 1853, John Jacob III had his horses hitched to his carriage and made the long and uncomfortable journey out of town to buy what was left of the Morris estate. He looked over the wooded hills, so confident in the future of the area that, on an impulse, he bent down and roughly marked on the cold, hard ground the places where building lots should go. This purchase was of the type his grandfather had made in his day. The Annexed District became the Bronx, one of the five boroughs of New York City.

This success did not excite John. How could it? Success is not exciting to one who has never failed.

As his father grew older, John Jacob took over more of the active management of the Estate. He was slightly more generous to his sublandlords than his father, and he did encourage them and the tenants to improve property—within limits. His true opinion of the houses put up by the sublandlords, though, is shown by his refusal to get fire insurance for them. As the city still depended on volunteer firemen, they often burned down.

"It is cheaper to lose a whole block of buildings by a fire every once in a while than to pay for an insurance policy," he would explain his position to his few intimate friends.

John Jacob Astor III

This would sometimes remind him of a story his father used to tell. William Backhouse had dashed home one day shouting: "Father, one of our houses on the Bowery is on fire!"

John Jacob I was studying the floor carefully and did not answer. William repeated his dramatic statement. His father bent down and picked something up. "Now that I have found the five-dollar bill I had dropped, you may tell me about that house. A bill in the hand is more important than a house in ashes."

John Jacob III would explain that this story was not really true. It had been told him to drive home an attitude that a good businessman should never forget.

Astor was indeed a good businessman, but when a foreign banker commented that it must be wonderful to have such a large fortune, he stroked his flowing side whiskers and replied gloomily: "Money brings me nothing but a certain dull anxiety."

One year seemed much like another to him, taking over the business from his aging, plodding father. The approach of the Civil War fired his enthusiasm in a way that real estate never had. From the very beginning he favored Lincoln, showing himself strong enough to oppose his father and pro-Southern Mayor Fernando Wood, whose good will was worth thousands of dollars. The one person who agreed with John wholeheartedly was his wife, although her family came from the South. Augusta was a woman of unusual character. She later encouraged the recruiting of a regiment of Negro troops and presented them with their flags herself.

Her husband was at his desk in the office of the Astor
Estate when the word came that Fort Sumter was be-
sieged by Southern troops demanding its surrender to
the state of South Carolina. Although he never showed
emotion outwardly, John Jacob was tremendously excited by the realization that this meant war. What was
his part in it to be?

The first thing he did was to give money. A letter
found in *Confederate Annals of the War* describes a conversation with General Robert E. Lee. "New York is
furnishing the Union government with large sums of
money," said Lee. "Astor is reported to have offered
ten million dollars." (The figure is probably an exag-
geration.)

But Astor could not endure remaining on the sidelines and so he decided to enter the Army. He did not
need to do so. This was a time before the draft and only
those men who wanted to enlist did so. Even in 1863
when the Union finally passed a draft law, anyone could
get out of serving by paying three hundred dollars or
finding a substitute. Enlistments and commissioning of
officers were somewhat casual in those early days of the
Civil War, and Astor simply had a uniform made for
him and reported to headquarters in late November of
1862.

With his imposing bearing and superb health, John
Jacob looked magnificent in his uniform. Although he
appeared every inch a soldier, the heir to Astor millions
was as raw a recruit as any to be found in the Army. His
years in the Astor Estate office could hardly be counted

as military training. Nonetheless, John was promptly given the rank of colonel. It was an era when no gentleman was expected to fight as a common soldier.

Astor was first assigned to Washington, D.C. Instead of living there in an Army camp, he rented a fine house and quickly hired a chef, steward, and valet to take care of him. The new colonel was to serve as an aide-de-camp to Major General George Brinton McClellan. This dashing young officer was a personification of the glamor of war in an era when war was still thought to be romantic. It has been said that no general was ever so loved by his soldiers, and Astor, too, was under his spell.

McClellan gave John Jacob a particularly sensible assignment for a man of his background.

"I have made it Colonel Astor's duty to remember and keep recorded all information in regard to transports, so that I may always know the exact condition of the transports and their locality," wrote McClellan.

Every ship, ferry, schooner, barge, and tugboat available was being gathered to carry McClellan's troops down the Potomac to the peninsula lying between the James and York rivers in Virginia. From there they were to march toward Richmond. It was still early in the war and there was a great deal of confusion, with plans changed from one day to the next. Astor was the very man to keep a clear head, no matter what was going on. In his apprenticeship to his father, he had learned how to change a tangled mass of information into a clear record. But he wanted action and this, too, was granted him and he followed his general up the peninsula.

"I was present at the siege of Yorktown and at the Battle of Williamsburgh, and took part in the Seven Days' fight or battles near Richmond," reported Astor.

Although McClellan's peninsular campaign ended in failure, Astor did not see it as such. He said later: "These have been the only exciting years of my life."

One of the soldiers who was with Colonel Astor in battle was amazed by the man's coolness: "If I had been the heir to the Astor fortunes and estate, I would have run away, if I had been hanged for it."

The Union Army was convinced that the Rebels picked off officers first. Some officers put on privates' uniforms to save themselves. John Jacob III never dreamed of doing so.

His father worried about him every second. "Where is Johann now?" he would mutter.

The family, gathered in the library at Rokeby, would be silent while William carefully read the accounts of the battles and studied the maps. He flatly forbade his younger son to join the Army at all. William, Jr., who had organized a regiment among the farmers in the area, was longing to fight. But he could not stand up to his father, and so he stayed home, while John was participating in the making of history.

One day an old friend of Astor's turned up in McClellan's camp. It was Fernando Wood, who was by then a leader of the pro-Southern underground Copperhead movement in the North. Wood's principles never stood

in the way of profit and he thought it only wise to pre-
pare for a possible Union victory by making friends
with the popular general. Wood suggested that McClellan might make an excellent Presidential candidate in
1864. The youthful McClellan was too flattered to realize that he should not have been with Wood at all.
Astor, used to seeing the success of Wood's underhanded
methods, was equally surprised by the objections that
the meeting aroused.

Despite his customary accuracy, Astor was exaggerat-
ing when he described his Army service as the "most
exciting years" of his life. He served only eight months.
By then he could see that McClellan's career was going
downhill, because of the failure to win the war. This
caused Astor to lose his enthusiasm for Army life. As he
was never formally commissioned, he was never actually
discharged. He just resigned from the Army in July of
1862 and went home. The following November Mc-
Clellan was relieved of his command.

John Jacob remained friends with McClellan and
offered him a position as president of the New Jersey
Railroad and Transport Company, controlled by the
Astors. The former general, however, wanted to run for
President in 1864, so he refused. It was not a wise de-
cision, as he lost badly.

Toward the end of the war, Astor was named brigadier general, an honorary commission. He preferred to
be known as "Colonel." For the rest of his life, he liked
to remember and talk about his Army days. Perhaps it

is a measure of his life that those eight months were all he was ever to know of excitement.

When Astor returned to New York in 1862, he found that the war had produced unrest in places far from the battlefields. Rebellion was in the North as well as in the South. The unfair draft law, which exempted the rich from military service, was the last straw, and in July of 1863 the slum dwellers rioted. They seized the Second Avenue armory and got possession of guns. For five days the rioters held off the police. Fifty buildings were burned and several hundred people killed or wounded. The riot was stopped only when the Seventh Regiment was brought back from the front. The draft riots frightened city officials and made people stop to think about the way the poor were living. Changing the draft law, as was done in 1864, could not be enough. Perhaps something basic should be done about the way the poor were living.

A Citizens Association was formed. John Jacob Astor III quickly realized that he was a citizen himself. He had himself put on the committee, along with another friendly citizen, his brother-in-law, the handsome Franklin H. Delano. The Association decided that a group of doctors should inspect the tenements.

None of the physicians who went on that tour was ever to forget what he saw. Five families shared a single room, taking turns at the two beds. In between turns, they sat on the floor or stood, as there were no chairs. No partitions or screens allowed the smallest amount of privacy. Staircases were so rickety that it was frightening to use them. Tenants rented and lived in cellar space only six feet high. The rooms upstairs were but seven or eight feet high, for that matter, and many had no light or ventilation of any kind. When a baby died of no apparent cause, the Bureau of Vital Statistics concluded that the death must have been due to "suffocation in the foul air of an apartment." Children were sent out into the streets at night to get a breath of air. Filth and vermin were everywhere. The sick lay with the well. Although the Croton Reservoir had brought running water into the city as early as 1842, the slum dwellers of the 1860's had none. Even the newer buildings in the Astor lots along First Avenue had only backyard toilets. At best one might find "school sinks" where water was turned on once or twice a day. A horrible stench from the garbage-filled gutters was in the air.

These findings horrified all New Yorkers, including the landlords. The doctors added to their concern by pointing out that, aside from the misery, it was impossible to control the epidemics of smallpox, cholera, and typhoid, so long as the crowded slums existed. All agreed that what was needed was a city board of health, and in 1866 one was organized.

"Some of the tenements are owned by persons of the highest character, but they fail to appreciate the responsibility resting on them," declared the new Board of Health.

This was certainly true of Astor, who was a most honorable and upright man and religious besides. In church he handed around the collection plate. In his office he opposed every measure that might improve the condition of the poor.

The city government in 1867 ruled that new tenements could not be built as close together as the old ones had been. No building was to take up more than 60 per cent of a lot. What is more, windows—forty-six thousand of them—were to be cut in the inner rooms of the tenements already standing, and cellars were not to be rented as living quarters.

Astor and the other landlords immediately raised objections. These men were not inhuman; they did not like the conditions in the slums. What they simply could not see was that the horrible situation in the tenements had very much to do with them as owners or builders. It was caused by the tenants who were dirty, shiftless, drunken, and careless. As for improvements, these were simply wasted on such people. Time and again, a landlord would put up partitions and build indoor toilets only to have the tenants take them apart and sell them piece by piece.

After five years of pressure by the landlords, the legislature gave the Board of Health the power to change the tenement law. This sounds as if the landlords had lost, but quite the opposite was true. Without real government support, the Board of Health was helpless. Its members tried to force the powerful landlords to improve the tenements, but in many cases they failed. They had to stand by while tenements went up on ninety feet or more of a hundred-foot lot, blocking out the light and air of all neighboring buildings.

Every few years objections to conditions in the slums would grow so strong that a new committee of investigation would be appointed. But a study of lists of committee names shows that they were seldom so new as all that. Astor was on one committee after the other. Only one of these investigating committees produced anything of a practical nature and this was the design for a model tenement to be known thereafter as a "dumbbell" or "old-law" tenement. The main change was an airshaft five or six feet wide to run down the center of a building. This provided some air for the inner rooms, but only on the top floors. Garbage and trash settled at the bottom of the shaft, and smelled so bad that tenants on lower floors had to keep their windows shut.

On one occasion Astor did contribute to the $260,000 fund being collected by the Improved Dwellings Association to put up a number of good houses. Each room was to have a window, and indoor bathrooms were planned. The profit on these houses was limited to 5 per cent. Not many such houses were built. Astor earned far more on the worst of the tenements.

The landlords were also able to block slum-clearance measures for years. In this they were helped by a corrupt city government, ready to do anything in return for money.

By the late 1860's New York City had fallen under the control of William Marcy Tweed, better known as "Boss" Tweed. He was indeed the "boss" of the city and had considerable power in the state as well. Although he held a variety of posts—State Senator, commissioner or deputy commissioner of schools and public works—his real strength lay in his position as head of Tammany, the most powerful group in the Democratic party. He was able to select the men who would hold high public office and he chose those who were either corrupt or were weak enough to close their eyes to his thievery. In 1869 he was able to make John T. Hoffman, one of "his" men, Governor. On the city level, it was Tweed all the way. He controlled the Mayor, A. Oakey Hall, whom he liked to call "Elegant Oakey"; the Comptroller, Richard B. Connolly, whose nickname of "Slippery Dick" he did not like to hear, and the City Chamberlain, Peter Barr Sweeney. These men were known as the "Tweed Ring."

In two and a half years these officials robbed the city of forty-five million dollars. This is how they did it: If a company wanted to put up a city building, the president of it was told that he must submit two bills, one to the city, and one to the Ring. In this way twelve million dollars of the taxpayers' money was allotted for a new city courthouse, which cost only three million dollars to build. The city actually lost more than the forty-five million dollars taken outright. Taxes were reduced for Tweed's friends and the rights to city property were given to them for practically nothing. If all these things are added together, the amount New York City lost during Tweed's days of power totals two hundred million dollars.

John Jacob Astor III

Despite his power, people began to talk about the utter corruption of Tweed's Ring. The elections of 1870 were coming up, and Tweed became concerned about the increasingly unfavorable reports of his activities. It would be wise to quiet them once and for all. He needed the cloak of respectability. With this in mind, he gathered a group of the most respected men in the city and asked them to form a committee to investigate the city's books. His good friend, John Jacob Astor III, agreed to head this committee.

Astor was known as an upright man. Although he enjoyed Tweed's favor, there was not the smallest doubt of his personal honesty. He would not have stolen a penny. Wanting low taxes is not public spirited, but it is not corrupt either. John knew, of course, that Tweed, like Wood before him, had done a number of things that were wrong. But when Tweed came to him with this infamous suggestion, Astor agreed to it as a business necessity. Along with five other leading citizens, Astor put his name to a report saying that all financial affairs of the city "are administered in a correct and faithful manner."

The report was released to the newspapers two days before the election. The voters were so impressed by the importance of the men who signed it that the Tammany candidates won again.

The backing of prominent citizens saved Tweed once, but he was ruined in the end by a single mistake. He quarreled with one of his underlings—a man who knew where the true records of the Tweed Ring's activities were kept. In July of 1871 he delivered a complete set of these records to the *New York Times*. The newspaper ran these in daily installments for three weeks. Readers were stunned as they learned how fourteen million dollars was stolen on a single April day.

This exposure finished off the Tweed Ring, and Tweed eventually died in jail.

Astor's good name survived his involvement with Tweed. His fortune, based on his slum property, grew ever larger. The value of the tenements was further increased when a new kind of manufacturing business, the sweatshop, sprang up. "Sweatshop" is an unpleasant name for an unpleasant practice. It was a business in which the workers were paid the smallest possible amount of money for each hour worked or piece of work completed. To make enough to keep from starving, they "sweated" late into the light. The sweatshops were first seen during the Civil War when women were hired to make uniforms for soldiers. Many of them were widows and desperate for money, and their employers took full advantage of them. It was not until the 1880's, however, that sweatshops really became common, as the result of an enormous wave of immigration from southern and eastern Europe. These immigrants were for the most part penniless and they had come here with no training in any trade. Some of the Italians were actually in debt, because unscrupulous men had lent them money to come to America, telling them of wonderful jobs and high salaries.

Upon arriving in New York, they quickly learned the

true facts of city life for the poor in the late nineteenth century. Instead of a good job at high pay, the immigrant had to accept a place as a sweatshop worker for from $1.00 to $3.00 a day. Instead of good housing, he was found a bed in a tenement rooming house for $.25 a night. If he had a family, he had to struggle to pay a rent of between $7.50 and $10.00 a month for a tiny crowded apartment. A number of families made a few extra cents by sharing their already cramped quarters with roomers even poorer than they, able to pay only $.30 or at best $.65 rent a week. Although prices were low, wages were even lower in proportion, compared to today. Milk cost $.04 a quart, meat was $.12 a pound, and butter $.08 for a quarter-pound chunk. Sometimes the wife and children would work to help out, though they could earn little more than $.025 for an hour. The very poorest children had few hopes of bettering themselves; in one crowded tenement only seven went to school.

Many of the sweatshops were run in the tenements, because they were cheaper for the employer than factory space. This was true even though the rent charged him by the sublandlord was much higher than that paid by ordinary tenants. It was not uncommon for the sublandlord himself to start a sweatshop in a vacant apartment.

One day a doctor visiting a tenement stopped to talk to the tenant of a small, dark, inside room. All the time they were chatting, the man, his wife, and twelve-year-old son kept on at their work making cigars. On an impulse, the physician asked if they knew who owned the house. "Astor," replied the cigar maker bitterly. The doctor commented later that this was the only time he found a tenant who knew the name of the top landlord. Astor and the other big real-estate owners stayed far away from slum buildings and did not ask the sublandlords for details on how they made their money.

By the 1880's, only a few years after the death of William Backhouse, the Astor Estate was worth at least eighty million dollars, and the income from the rentals amounted to about five million dollars a year. John got half of this as the elder son, and his brother, William Backhouse, Jr., got a third. The other relatives divided the rest. John Jacob III sat at his desk while his agents came in to bring the reports of the rentals collected. One of them noticed his employer writing and rewriting a telegram one day. Astor was trying to find a way to save a word.

The account of the Astor Estate holdings was kept in big flat ledgers. A study of them reveals an Astor lot or building on almost any block in the city, selected at random. John Jacob Astor I and his sons and grandsons had indeed been right in their belief that the city would grow, chiefly northward, but in other directions as well. In many ways the new sprawling New York was a much uglier city than it had been in the days of the first of the Astors. Trash barrels overflowed their repellent contents on every street corner. Sidestreets were narrow and filthy. Even the tree-lined streets were pretty only in the spring, as the city employed just a handful of street cleaners, and they did not have time to rake leaves. The

homeowners should have, but few of them did. Houses
had gone up so fast that beauty had been sacrificed.
Rows of buildings, one just like the other, stood side
by side. Central Park recalled the loveliness of earlier
days, but even there any stroller who looked around
could see the ramshackle cabins of squatters on the
nearby hillsides.

At least it was easier to get around the city. In 1870
steam locomotives pulled railway cars along tracks built
on platforms above the streets all the way up to Thirti-
eth Street, and by 1888, the elevated railway lines had
been extended to 169th Street. Passengers traveling to
such a distant point could look down on the country
estates of the rich and the cabbage and poultry farms of
the poor. For a time the Third Avenue elevated maintained a special car for rich people at double fare.
Wealthy men, like the Astors, did not really like to sit
with the poor from whom they made most of their
money.

Whatever can be said against the way in which the
Astor fortune was earned, there can be no question that
Augusta Astor, the wife of John Jacob Astor III, used
as much of it as possible in doing good. A magazine
writer expressed the view of the time in describing her
as a "woman of exceptionally beautiful character."

"Augusta really wanted to help everyone she came in
contact with," a friend said of her. "If her dressmaker
looked upset, she would find out what was the matter
and then do something about it."

She presented $225,000 for the Astor Pavilion, first

building of the Memorial Hospital for the treatment of cancer. Her favorite charity was a project run by the new Children's Aid Society to send poor boys from the slums to foster homes on farms in the Midwest. With whole families starving in overcrowded rooms, little boys wandered in the streets hunting for something to eat, sell, or steal. The Children's Aid program saved at least a few of them from a life of hunger and crime. Some of the boys, it was later learned, were treated badly, but at that time no other efforts were being made for them. During her lifetime Mrs. John Jacob Astor III paid the way for about fifteen hundred of these youngsters.

As a group of boys was about to leave, Augusta would appear at the train station, a small, frail figure almost overbalanced by a large hat pinned atop her coronet braids. She would rush up and down the line of boys, the jeweled cross she wore on a chain around her neck swinging wildly, as she made sure that each had received her gift of a coat, hat, scarf, shoes, and gloves. One day she noticed that something was missing.

"And your Testaments, boys?" she asked.

They were quite willing to go without the Bibles, but she would not hear of it. While they stood waiting, she dashed over to Bible House to get the books.

John Jacob III, who was public spirited in anything not connected with business, supported her in these charities and after her death gave a lot of money to the Children's Aid Society for a school to be run in her memory.

But to show Augusta as an earnest giver of charity is to miss all the gaiety and charm of her nature. After the death of her father-in-law in 1875, Augusta had blossomed out and become one of the city's leading hostesses. She had an original mind and did not follow the rules of the society of her day. Edwin Booth, younger brother of the man who had assassinated Lincoln, was not being received by anyone else in society. Augusta Astor had him to dinner and gave him the place of honor on her right.

Not content with giving balls, she started a literary circle. Each of the forty prominent society matron members was required to write a story, essay, or poem and read it aloud to the group. Mrs. Astor's compositions are not to be found among the family papers. But then, there are surprisingly few family papers.

When the Astors moved their office uptown to 21-23 West Twenty-sixth Street, John Jacob III came to watch over the packing. To the surprise of the workmen, he insisted that all old books and documents be burned.

"He did it to save the cost of moving them," muttered one of the workmen. John's economies were well known by then.

His friends, though, believed that he did it because he feared that the records might fall into the hands of reporters. He had a terror of publicity.

"He was even afraid to write letters," remarked one of them. "I only got two or three from him in all the time I knew him. He begged me to burn them after I finished reading them."

This attitude had been passed down to him by his father. When John Jacob I had died, William Backhouse Astor deliberately destroyed fifteen packing cases filled with old papers. A part of history vanished in the flames.

4

The Mrs. Astor
and the Making of Society

SHE WAS NEITHER beautiful nor brilliant; her manner
lacked charm and her conversation wit. The husband,
whom she said she loved, ignored her, often fleeing from
her side. But no one seeing her standing in purple velvet, with her small plump body held stiffly erect to
counterbalance the weight of a fortune in jewels could
have missed knowing that he was in the presence of one
of the great personalities of an era.

This woman, Caroline Webster Schermerhorn Astor,
was to become so well-known that to this day the name
"*the* Mrs. Astor" can mean no one else. The world that
she ruled was not the world of business dominated by
the family she had married into; it was not the world
of politics and government, or that of literature and the
arts. Today it is hard to believe that a woman could become so famous simply by being the ruler of society.

Yet in the nineteenth century there was little else that a woman of ambition could do. The day of the career woman had not dawned. Limited though her goals may have been, Caroline made more of a mark on New York than the bright, charming, but weak man she married.

At the time of the marriage, though, friends of William Backhouse Astor, Jr., wondered why he had ever agreed to marry this dull, homely girl, with the big nose, small mouth, and heavy jaw, who was still single at twenty-two. And in 1853 a girl that old was well on the way to being a spinster. William, for his part, was not only the heir to a great fortune, but was a most appealing young man besides. After his brilliant showing at Columbia, William had traveled in Egypt, Palestine, Turkey, and Greece and learned a great deal about their art and literature. The trip had given him broad interests in an era when most rich men, his brother included, had little to talk about outside of business. His cultured taste and polished manners were a striking contrast to the heavy cold correctness of his father and brother. Caroline had no way of knowing in advance that she had gotten a second-best Astor. No one warned her that nothing William was or did could make up in his father's eyes for the fact that he was not the eldest son. Whenever he would come to the Astor Estate office, his father and brother, John, would look up coldly. Feeling unwanted, he left. It was enough to drive a man to drink . . . and it did.

Caroline may have been upset by her husband's failings, but she tried not to show it. Instead she did what

ohn Jacob Astor I, who arrived in this country penniless and became the
chest man in America. After portrait by E. D. Marchant.

Hellgate, the country estate of John Jacob Astor I, located far from the cit
on what is now 88th Street and Second Avenue.

The area that became downtown New York was a pleasant, sleepy country
side when John Jacob Astor I first saw it.

William Backhouse Astor, as a boy, from an old miniature treasured by his descendants.

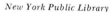

lliam Backhouse Astor, the n. He grew up in his father's dow, but doubled the fortune l was landlord of New York. m a portrait by Eastman nson.

John Jacob Astor II, who insanity was the tragedy ⬦ his father's life.

Eliza Astor von Rumpff. She was her father's favorite, a gentle, religious girl who died young.

ohn Jacob Astor III. His
huge fortune brought him
"nothing but a certain dull
anxiety." From a portrait
after Madrazo.

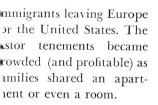

Immigrants leaving Europe
for the United States. The
Astor tenements became
crowded (and profitable) as
families shared an apart-
ment or even a room.

The Metropolitan Museum of Art, Gift of Orme Wilson and R. Thornton Wilson, 1949.

The Mrs. Astor stood beneath this portrait by Carolus-Duran while greeting her guests.

William Backhouse Astor, Jr., the charming man whose forceful wife refused to use either his first or middle name.

The art-gallery ballroom where *the* Mrs. Astor entertained the "Four Hundred."

In the 1860's pigs, chickens, and goats still grazed in front of the ramshackle frame houses that lay East of 42nd Street.

The Astor House, first of the great hotels built by this family, was visited by Abraham Lincoln, Edgar Allan Poe, Charles Dickens, and other politicians and celebrities.

John Jacob Astor IV, his son Vincent, and friends enjoy an afternoon at Newport, favorite resort for generations of Astors.

Ava Astor in a rare display of affection to her little daughter Alice.

Harper's Bazaar

Fifth Avenue and 65th Street. *The* Mrs. Astor and her son John Jacob Astor IV lived in the house on the corner, which had cost $1,500,000 to build and another $750,000 to furnish.

Byron Collection, Museum of the City of New York

The Astor Library on Lafayette Place. The one great charity of John Jacob Astor I, it was supported thereafter by his descendants.

The Croton Reservoir at Fifth Avenue and 42nd Street. It was later moved to make room for the New York Public Library, which included the Astor Library.

William Waldorf Astor, who left America to become a British aristocrat—first a baron and then a viscount.

Mrs. William Waldorf Astor, the former Mary Paul. Her husband wanted to make her *the* Mrs. Astor.

Cliveden, the magnificent country estate, first owned by the Duke of Buckingham-shire in 1666. It was bought by William Waldorf Astor and became a social and political center for three generations of Englishmen.

Lord William Waldorf Astor, the third viscount, leading his prize-winning racehorse. After his sudden death in 1966, the Astors moved out of Cliveden.

An Astor family group in England. (Standing, left to right) William Waldorf, Viscount Waldorf Astor, Robert Gould Shaw III (Lady Astor's son by her first marriage); (seated) David, Michael, Lady Nancy Astor, John Jacob VII, and Phyllis.

John Jacob Astor VI and his first wife, the former Ellen Tuck French, after their wedding. Their son was given the second of the traditional family names—William Backhouse Astor.

Vincent Astor on the deck of his yacht, *Nourmahal*. The animals are being brought back from the Galapagos Islands in the Pacific.

she could to make her forceful personality felt in the family. Greenwich Village, she insisted, was no longer fashionable. In fact, Astor Place, which had been the scene of a slum riot back in 1849, had never lost its nickname of "Massacre Place." It was really not an area in which to bring up children, and Mrs. Astor planned, indeed had to have, more, as she had so far produced only a daughter. After carefully weighing the real-estate holdings of her husband's family, she settled on the old Thompson Farm at Thirty-fourth Street and Fifth Avenue which her father-in-law had bought years earlier. Pushed by Caroline, William summoned up his courage and asked his father for half of the property. Once suggested, it was so obviously an ideal place to live that John Jacob III and Augusta decided to build themselves a mansion on the other half of the plot, giving Caroline the satisfaction of having for once imposed her will on the entire Astor family. Twin four-story red brick houses went up side by side, joined by a garden and protected from the eyes of passers-by, with a high wall.

Fifth Avenue was very different from a fashionable block of today. The street was badly paved with irregular stones. A drive up the Avenue left the traveler shaken. In fact, one society doctor refused to let delicate ladies go driving at all. Even so, the Astors were quickly joined on Fifth Avenue by the Vanderbilts and other rich New Yorkers.

In the northern of the two Astor buildings, Caroline

gave birth to three more daughters and a son. Caroline found her greatest joy in her children.

"She was one of those women to whom one instinctively applies the adjective 'motherly' in no matter what walk of life they may be placed," wrote a friend.

This was fortunate, as William even then was out more than he was home, preferring gayer and prettier companions to his wife. He had quickly realized that Caroline was more forceful than he and that she would bully him as his father had. Discouraged, he responded in the only way he knew—withdrawal. He built an estate, Ferncliff, outside the city and when not leading the gay life, devoted his energies to running a farm and breeding race horses. Caroline joined him there occasionally, and at Easter they often went to Europe together. For the most part, though, the relationship of husband and wife was distant: as he pushed her out of his life, she, in turn, pushed him out of the lives of their children.

Although Caroline always felt important, she did not set herself the task of organizing society until the 1870's when her eldest daughter, Caroline, turned eighteen. At this point, she looked around carefully, and she was horrified by the change in society.

The Civil War had brought a revolution in customs, morals, and social behavior in the North as well as the South. Mrs. Astor found that society was not the way it had been when she was a young girl, moving in the highest circles as a member of a socially prominent family of Dutch origin. In those days, everyone in society knew everyone else. By the 1870's this had ceased to be true. The city had simply grown too large as a result of the arrival of many Southerners and the continuing immigration from Europe. It was no longer even possible, Mrs. Astor complained, to know everyone who was rich. The Astors had not been the only people to get richer during the war. While some fortunes had been lost, others were won. And in a city ruled by Boss Tweed, some vicious and corrupt men had become wealthy. Caroline was particularly concerned by a lowering of moral standards, by wild parties, gambling, drinking, and vice.

She wanted to be sure that her daughters would be safe as they began to move in the social life of the city. In particular, she wanted them to know those people of whom she personally approved, people with backgrounds as good (or nearly as good) as hers. This could only be achieved, she saw, if she took a firm hand and organized society along the lines she thought proper, by bringing together members of the families she knew, and keeping out all newcomers.

Caroline Astor's dream could never have become reality without the help of a little man with thin hair, a developing paunch, and a carefully shaped beard. Ward McAllister had come to New York from Savannah, Georgia, with the fervent wish to devote his life to creating a society here that was as formal as that of European royalty. It was a strange ambition for a man, but it was to prove valuable to Mrs. Astor. In time she was to be known as the "queen" of society, and he as her "prime minister."

In order to show the world just whom they considered worthy of membership in their narrow social realm, they formed a special organization, the Patriarchs, which was to have no activities outside of giving balls. The Patriarchs was so exclusive a group that only twenty-five men were asked to be members. These gentlemen were not all there was of society, but they (and their wives) knew everyone else who was and these select few were to be invited to the balls.

The original group of Patriarchs contained a rather large number of Astors, Schermerhorns, and their connections, which surely came as no surprise to anyone in the fashionable Thirties on Fifth Avenue. Later, when vacancies occurred, McAllister and Mrs. Astor checked the backgrounds of applicants, although, of course, they really knew everyone who counted already. Neither of them accepted either Jews or Catholics as members. Society was prejudiced against people belonging to either faith.

Mrs. Astor did not overlook the fact that her daughters were her main reason for organizing society, and so she and McAllister arranged the Family Circle dancing classes for young girls. Ward had a personal interest—his homely daughter, Louise. He happily described the dancing classes as "Junior Patriarchs," and they were indeed a preparation for marriage to the very kind of man who was sure to become a senior Patriarch.

Those members of society who belonged to the Patriarchs and sent their children to the Family Circle spent their money in a way that would be thought vulgar today. At one dinner party in the 1870's, for example, each male guest received as a favor a cigar rolled in a hundred-dollar bill with the host's initials inscribed in gold. At another a thirty-foot-long pond with four swans brought in from Brooklyn's Prospect Park was set up in the center of the floor of a fashionable restaurant. The swans, sad to say, behaved very badly, although they had been drugged. In Caroline Astor's home, every wish was attended to by a large staff of servants dressed in blue uniforms that were an exact copy of those worn in the royal palace in England. Dinners lasting three hours or longer were served on heavy gold plates, and the table was always covered with hundreds of hothouse roses which cost a dollar apiece, or with orchids.

French cooking was favored for the nine-course meals that included soup, a fish course, at least two main meat courses, several in-between courses of mousse or sherbet, cheeses, and desserts. A slender figure was not then in style.

The clothing was flamboyant in an era when rich people were supposed to look rich. The father of a young girl in the Astors' social set told of spending twenty thousand dollars to dress his daughter for a single New York season. This sum provided forty-five gowns, seven coats and cloaks, forty-eight lace-embroidered chemises, and twenty pearl-encrusted hair nets. Mrs. Astor dressed like a queen in white satin embroidered with pearls and silver, trailing a train of green velvet, or in her favorite purple velvet trimmed with pale blue satin and embroidered with gold beads. Her gowns were so heavily covered with beading and jewels, both front and back, that it was impossible for her to lean back in a chair.

"I only remember her in evening clothes covered with diamonds," murmurs an old lady, recalling that golden era.

At one ball she wore a triple necklace of diamonds, a diamond brooch said to have belonged to the ill-fated French queen Marie Antoinette, a twelve-row fall of diamonds over the bosom of her dress, a diamond tiara, and diamond stars in her black hair, or rather her wig, as Mrs. Astor was not satisfied with her own hair.

Every Monday Mrs. Astor attended the opera. The Academy of Music, which had been opened in 1854, had one drawback that in time became critical: It had only eighteen boxes in all. This was not even enough for the Patriarchs, and people paid up to thirty thousand dollars to get one. In 1883–84 a new opera house was opened, with enough boxes to please the very rich. The boxes of the Metropolitan Opera House soon became known as the "Diamond Horseshoe," because of the jewels worn by the ladies occupying them. Many people said that it was really named in honor of Mrs. Astor's diamonds. Opera glasses from all over the house were focussed on Caroline in Box Number Seven, seated with McAllister or other friends (hardly ever with her husband). She would not leave her seat during intermission, remaining there to receive her many admirers. But Mrs. Astor could seldom stay to the end of the last aria, as balls were usually held on Mondays, too. Nothing was more important to Mrs. Astor than a ball—her own or those of the other social leaders.

Mrs. Astor's largest ball of the year, held on one of the first three Mondays in January, was considered the high point of the social season. In addition to this one, she gave an endless procession of dinners, parties, and lesser balls, many of them attended by several hundred people. The arriving guests would be greeted by the queenly hostess, standing alone or with her grown children beneath a portrait of herself painted by Carolus Duran. They would then go to the great ballroom where the walls were covered with paintings by well-known artists of the day. These were hung one on top of the other, as if in a museum, rather than a home. At 1:30 A.M. came the moment in the evening to which everyone looked forward, when the german or cotillion with its intricate steps was performed. The guests were rewarded with favors for their efforts—flowers for the buttonholes of the men and brooches, bracelets, necklaces, or long jeweled hairpins for the ladies.

Sometimes, with a hint of malice, a guest would express surprise at the fact that Mr. Astor was absent. There would be a hush while others in the crowded room waited to see how Mrs. Astor would react. Caroline never lost her air of calm. "Oh, he is having a delightful cruise on his yacht. The sea air is good for him," she would remark. "It is a great pity I am such a poor sailor, for I should so much enjoy accompanying him."

William was one of the great yachtsmen of his day,

possessing first a sailing yacht, *Ambassadress,* and later the largest steam yacht of the period, the *Nourmahal,* which means "light of the harem." On one or another of these boats, William liked to put the length of the continent between him and his wife. While she was occupying herself with ruling New York society, he was living on board his yacht, anchored off the coast of Florida. Founding the Florida Yacht Club, he became its first commodore. Florida had not yet become a resort, and the governor was delighted to welcome a member of such a prominent family. In addition, William was charming to everyone and was every bit as sought after in Florida as his wife was in New York. The governor, looking for ways to keep William happy, invited him to join the military staff. Astor was so pleased that he paid for a company of soldiers to search the Everglades, as hostile Indians were believed to be hiding there. The state in return made Astor a present of eighty thousand acres.

In New York William left real-estate planning first to his father and then his brother because they kept telling him he had no head for business. But in Florida his confidence was greater and he invested ten thousand dollars in a large plot of ground in Jacksonville and then had the three-story Astor Building put up with his name in iron letters on top. Showing what looked like Astor foresight, he bought fourteen thousand acres in Orange County near Jacksonville for only seven thousand-five hundred dollars and talked about planting the largest orange grove in the world. Nearby he built a fourteen-room hotel, a store, and a large dock, and the town was promptly named "Astor" in his honor. But somehow nothing ever worked out well for William. Any of the other Astors would have made a fortune. Many orange growers were to become wealthy in that very county. But William's groves never did well, and the dock was nearly destroyed by fire. His land dropped in value year after year. It was finally sold by his grandson in 1938 for just thirty-one hundred dollars. Still, the towns of Astor and Astor Park remain as a tribute to the Astor who hated New York's formal society.

Nonetheless, William had enough of a sense of family, an Astor trait, to return when something he considered important—not his wife's parties—occurred.

Caroline would take each of these opportunities to tell her friends: "Dear William is so good to me. I have been so fortunate in my marriage."

Such an event was the engagement of his daughter Emily in the winter of 1875–76 to James J. Van Alen. Although Van Alen's father had been a cavalry commander in the Civil War and was an investor in the New York Central Railroad, William did not approve of him and made such nasty remarks that Van Alen challenged him to a duel. William was eventually talked into sending a letter of apology. He even brought himself to give the bride away and to stand by his wife's side at the reception at home, but late in the afternoon he reached the limit of his always limited endurance and fled to his yacht to set sail for Florida at once. Emily, like the aunt whose name she had been given, died young in childbirth, leaving three motherless babies.

In 1878 her younger sister, Helen, married James Roosevelt Roosevelt (yes, this Roosevelt made his name doubly sure), stepson of Sara Delano Roosevelt and half brother of Franklin Delano Roosevelt. The third of Mrs. Astor's daughters, Charlotte Augusta, named after her aunt, married James Coleman Drayton of Philadelphia the following year. This left the Astors with just two young children, Caroline and John Jacob IV, at home.

Every summer the family—with the frequent exception of William—went to a cottage in Newport, Rhode Island. This seaside community has long been known for its healthful climate. In 1783 George Washington had urged an ailing nephew to go there. Until the mid-nineteenth century Newport was popular with Southerners trying to escape the heat. The resort was very quiet then, as can be seen by the form of exercise most popular with the Southern belles. Chairs were attached to each end of a "joggle board," a kind of seesaw. Young ladies would joggle one another up and down by pushing with their pretty little feet.

Newport had become considerably livelier by the time the Astors settled down there for "the season." A Newport cottage is in reality a French chateau or Italian Renaissance-style mansion, costing several million dollars to build, and as much or even more to fill with marble sculpture, original paintings, imported French carpets, cutglass chandeliers, and heavy carved furniture. Mrs.

Astor's cottage was Beechwood, and right nearby was Beaulieu, the castle owned by the John Jacob Astor III's.

There has never been—and never again could be—another place like Newport in the late nineteenth century. The people who spent the summers there were convinced that they were truly superior to everyone else. Street cars were routed away from the homes of the prominent, by request of the Astors.

"If you were not of the inner circle," McAllister wrote in an odd little book that gave advice on entering society, "and were a new-comer, it took the combined efforts of all your friends backing and pushing to procure an invitation for you."

There was indeed no place where a newcomer was made to feel more inferior. The natives of Newport were no better off. Even their beach, Easton's, was known to socialites as "the Common Beach." The insiders bathed at Bailey's Beach, protected from the uninvited by a watchman wearing a uniform with gold lacing. The ladies sat on the beach dressed in heavy flannel bathing suits with skirts hanging to below their knees, stockings, bathing shoes, and a straw bonnet. Sunburn was considered low class. The bathing suits were designed to protect modesty. When wet, they were so heavy that they actually brought danger of drowning. The most athletic of the girls played tennis at the Casino, feeling incredibly daring without their corsets. Through most of the 1880's, though, heavy petticoats were still worn beneath a long, tight tennis gown with a flounce at the bottom. The men players came out on the court in brightly striped flannel jackets which they removed before playing, long gray trousers, and a small cap with a brim.

The older ladies and those who disliked active sports strolled slowly in the mornings near the Casino listening to a stringed band and showing off their clothes. Just because they were at the beach did not mean that proper dress was neglected. Mrs. Astor and her fellow matrons and their daughters changed their dresses several times a day, and brought a wardrobe of at least ninety gowns to "the country." Each daytime dress had a matching hat and parasol. The hats had wide brims and were decorated with feathers. They were carefully pinned on the hair that had first been padded out with wiglets, then known by the unpleasant name of "rats." The summer's heat was considered no reason to leave off white elbow-length kid gloves in daytime or evening and a popular lady might run through three or four fresh pairs a day. Even at a clambake gloves were worn until the actual moment when the clams were brought to the table in tin basins.

Every day after lunch a parade of ladies in horse-drawn carriages driven by uniformed coachmen set off. The matrons would nod or smile at one another, pretending not to notice the townspeople staring at them. And in a society ruled by Mrs. Astor, no lady dared to overtake the carriage of one with superior social rank.

The days were filled with dressing, bathing, dressing, tennis, dressing, lunch, driving, resting, and dressing again, and the nights were filled with elaborate balls. An intimate evening at home with Caroline Astor would find one dining with a hundred other guests.

Although most of New York and Newport considered her to be queen of society, Caroline was not satisfied. The Astors had to know it, too. There were at this time two other Mrs. Astors in Newport—her older sister-in-law, Augusta, and the wife of her nephew, William Waldorf Astor. Nonetheless, she was, she decided, *the* Mrs. Astor and she cut her husband's name from her calling cards. Her friends were told that all mail from then on was to be addressed to "Mrs. Astor, Newport." Mrs. John Jacob Astor III was only amused by this and cheerfully continued to use her full name, but her son had no sense of humor and was enraged. He insisted that his shy, beautiful wife, Mary Paul, was *the* Mrs. Astor, and he, too, gave orders to this effect to friends and postmen. This resulted in a good deal of mixed-up mail, but nothing else. Mary did not have either the character or the desire to battle her aunt. Caroline Astor won a decisive victory for all time, and the name by which she was then and forever after known to the world was as "*the* Mrs. Astor."

With Mrs. Astor in firm command, acceptance by the inner circle of society meant acceptance by her. And so she was suspicious of the motives of any young man who came calling on her daughter Caroline. The girl bore no resemblance to her mother; blonde and slight, she was the very sweetest of the Astor children. In 1884 she fell in love with young Orme Wilson. The Astors—and

William for once agreed with his wife—raised objections and said that Orme's father would have to settle half a million dollars on the young couple, a figure that the Astors would then match. This was obviously unfair, as William Astor could easily afford that amount and Wilson could not. The groom's father, after considerable soul-searching, finally agreed. Despite this, Mrs. Astor remained unenthusiastic until the spring day when she saw the young sweethearts coming out of church together hand in hand, looking at one another tenderly. At that moment she became convinced that Orme loved her daughter truly and not just for money and social position. From that day on she threw herself wholeheartedly into plans for a great wedding, and the bride walked down an aisle set up in the huge ballroom at 350 Fifth Avenue, her little feet cushioned from the hard dance floor by a three-inch-thick carpet. The guest list included former President Ulysses S. Grant.

The next big wedding in the family took place in 1891 when John Jacob Astor IV married—with the full approval of both parents—Ava Lowle Willing, a devastating beauty of Philadelphia and Newport, whose family claimed descent from Alfred the Great, Henry I, Edward I, Henry III and Henry IV of England, and Henry I of France. The very rich groom gave his fairly rich bride a diamond tiara on which to fasten her veil, while his mother presented a four-inch-large lovers' knot also made of diamonds.

Newspapers from coast to coast wrote about this, as well as everything else that went on in the mansions lining Fifth Avenue. Mrs. Astor, like most of her family, could not endure publicity—as she grew older she would not go near the Fifth Avenue windows of her home unless the curtains were drawn—but she was quite unable to avoid it. Gossip columns about society had been steadily gaining in popularity. A debutante visiting an aunt in Montana was able to impress ranchers and their wives by telling them that she had attended one of Mrs. Astor's balls. Her listeners, she learned, already knew that Mrs. Astor had worn a green velvet, gold-embroidered gown.

In the newspapars of the nation the high society group came to be known as "the 400." No one is sure where this term originated, but there appears little question that McAllister made it popular. In addition to living the society life, he wrote about it, and his articles, which were widely reprinted, were full of anecdotes about the 400. How did he arrive at that figure? Some said that he meant the number which could fit into Mrs. Astor's ballroom, but that is simply not true. The vast room held 800 or more on many occasions.

When persistent reporters asked him to name the 400, he hemmed and hawed, but eventually, in 1892, gave the official list of those invited to Mrs. Astor's major ball of the year to the *New York Times.* It included the Chanlers, Vanderbilts, Mills, Livingstons, Goelets, Fishes, Delafields, Cushings, Jays, Rhinelanders, and De Peysters. But by a peculiar quirk of fate, Mrs. Astor gave a particularly small ball that year. And so that famous "four hundred" list contained just 220 different names;

the figure can be raised to 309 only by counting each "and Mrs." as a separate entry.

Whether two hundred, three hundred, or four hundred rightly belonged in the inner circle, its center was Mrs. Astor. She always insisted on the most proper and conventional behavior, and so it came as a terrible blow to her when her daughter Charlotte Augusta Drayton left her husband and children to run away to Paris with another man. To Mrs. Astor's intense embarrassment, the newspapers gave full accounts of the romance. One of them even published Augusta's love letters.

Her father warned Augusta that if she did not return to her husband, he would cut her out of his will and have all her possessions up to and including her childhood toys and wedding dress sold at auction. In the midst of the crisis, when the family was gathered in Paris trying to talk reason to Augusta, William suddenly exclaimed: "I've got an awful pain." Two days later he was dead.

These were black years for *the* Mrs. Astor. A year after William's death, her daughter Helen Roosevelt died suddenly. As for Augusta, after being divorced by Drayton and losing custody of her children, she decided she was tired of her sweetheart. Instead she married a handsome and rich young Scotsman, George Ogilvie Haig. *The* Mrs. Astor, during the entire scandal, had showed her true mettle, remaining loyal to her daughter. Her posture was a little more queenly, her bejeweled head held a little higher; that was all.

After William's death, Caroline Astor moved to a magnificent mansion at Sixty-fifth Street and Fifth Avenue. It was designed to be a double-house, divided by a removable partition, because she wanted her adored son John and his family to live with her. By the time the house was finished, Mrs. Astor had invested a million-and-a-half dollars in the building and another three-quarters of a million in furnishings selected to make each room represent a different period.

Her living expenses were high, too. She had a large staff of servants, and a butler at this time received seventy-five dollars a month and footmen were paid fifty-five dollars each, provided they agreed to wear uniforms and powder their hair. The chef of an Astor or Vanderbilt could command a hundred dollars a month and 10 per cent of the food bills—often five hundred dollars a month to the butcher and one hundred twenty-five dollars to the grocer. Servants in homes of people less wealthy than these received but a fraction of those salaries—eighteen to twenty dollars a month for a cook and twelve to fifteen dollars for a maid.

Ward McAllister died in 1895 and his place was taken by Harry Lehr, who was quite another type of prime minister. Lehr had approached Mrs. Astor as he approached all of life, as a comedian. The wealthy Baltimore family into which he was born lost its money when he was a boy and Harry determined to get it back, but not by anything so dull as work. His big opportunity came when he was invited to a party in Newport attended by Mrs. Astor. She was always a-glitter with diamonds, and so he seized a huge bouquet of flowers out of a vase and thrust them upon her, saying, "Here, you look like a walking chandelier." His manner was so merry and he was so young—younger than her son—that Mrs. Astor was charmed, instead of being offended. She invited him to lead her next cotillion and he began, as he put it, "to scale the heights." Within weeks he had gained the title of "society's court jester."

Lehr was soon involved in a number of pranks that startled Mrs. Astor. He brought a circus elephant into the mansion of one of her friends and had guests feed the animal peanuts as they danced by. One banquet was arranged for a hundred dogs, and at another male guests were instructed to dress as cats and were then handed white mice to present to the ladies. His most startling idea was a dinner said to be in honor of a visiting Prince Del Drago. The prince was late, so the other guests were already at the table when he arrived on Lehr's arm and was led to the chair usually occupied by Mrs. Astor, who was fortunately absent. Del Drago turned out to be a nice little monkey neatly dressed in a full set of evening clothes.

It was becoming clear that Mrs. Astor had lost the ability to keep the tight control on society that had characterized her during the previous twenty years. Even at home she was less strict in her requirements. In 1904, twelve hundred guests were invited to her ball. One newspaper in distress wrote: "She lets Bars 'Way Down and Asks Even the Edge of the Fringe of Society." Her guests spilled drinks on her sofas, burned table tops with cigars, and struck matches on the walls.

It was nearly the end. By 1906 she had stopped going out or inviting others to her home. For the last two years of her life, rumors about her were passed through society in New York, Newport, and the rest of the nation. Her mind, and this at least is true, was affected, possibly by a stroke, or old age, or simply by the tragedies in her personal life. These could well have broken as unbending a nature as hers. People said that she wandered about the house (although other reports had her confined to a wheel chair) talking to the ghosts of her past: William, whose love she had not possessed and whose wandering spirit she had not been able to tame; Charlotte Augusta whose stormy, passionate life had cast a blot on her own record of correctness; Emily dead in childbirth after only five years of the marriage William had so vigorously opposed; Helen, too, dead so soon after her father.

A legend sprang up that during these last years, queenly in posture still, she would dress in her finest purple velvet and stand in the reception room, bowing to imaginary guests, though this last seems a bit unlikely. The doctor, two nurses, three maids, and butler who cared for her to the end held their tongues.

Shortly before she withdrew from social life, Mrs. Astor had granted one of the few newspaper interviews she ever gave. "I am not vain enough to believe that New York will not be able to get along without me," she declared with dignity. "Many women will rise up to fill my place."

Caroline was wrong. In the world of society, at least, no one then or in the years since has ever been able to replace *the* Mrs. Astor.

5

William Waldorf Astor,
the First Aristocrat

"HF HAD BEEN madly in love, but his parents discovered that there was tuberculosis in the girl's family and they did not let him marry her," said the grandson of William Waldorf Astor. "I think this affected him all his life with a sort of nostalgia and longing."

Many people alive today still remember Astor vividly. Their memories, however, are of the unconventional and overpowering personality he became in old age, rather than the soulful young man he once was. They describe him in cutaway coat, top hat, flannel trousers, and sneakers, not caring any more how he looked. And yet in his youth, he had been strikingly handsome, with brilliant blue eyes, blond hair and mustache, and ruddy complexion. Well over six feet tall (some accounts put him at six feet, four inches), his build was powerful and muscular and his bearing military. "In the end he seemed an almost inaccessible person," wrote a friend after his death, "an imprisoned soul immured within walls of his own making." Yes, it is hard to imagine this forbidding presence as ever having been young and in love.

A suitable marriage was arranged for William with Mary Dahlgren Paul, the lovely Philadelphia girl who was to prove so unequal to her struggle with her husband's aunt, *the* Mrs. Astor. Mamie, as she was called, with her liquid dark eyes and long gleaming black hair, was much sought after by the young bachelors of Newport and Philadelphia. But Mamie was never lucky. Her beauty, shyness, and perfect manners would surely have won any man whose heart was not engaged elsewhere. "It was not a happy marriage," says an old lady who knew them. She lowers her voice: "He was not nice to live with." Even before her social defeat at the hands of *the* Mrs. Astor, Mamie was sadly aware of the fact that her husband was disappointed in the marriage.

Finding a way to burn up his limitless energy was a lifelong problem for this ambitious, discontented, and imaginative man. He had never gone to college, but had been tutored privately at home and in Europe. This method provided him with a good education, but encouraged his sense of superiority and he was never able to get along with others. He joined his father in the Astor Estate office and did what was expected of him, but he hated it. Luckily his father did not object when William Waldorf expressed interest in a career in politics.

William Waldorf Astor

Despite the Astors' involvement (viewed by them as strictly business) with Tammany's Boss Tweed, the family had been Republican since the Civil War and had actively supported Ulysses S. Grant. This proved rather helpful to William's budding political career, because the New York Republican party machine was dominated by Grant's good friend, Roscoe Conkling.

With this backing, Astor, aged twenty-nine, was nominated and elected to the New York State Senate. "I do not go in the interests of any class, but for the city's good," he declared piously.

During his first term he voted the same way as his party leaders, and was duly re-elected. In his second term, though, he introduced a bill to reduce the ten-cent fare for the New York elevated train to five cents. The elevated was controlled by August Belmont, Russell Sage, and Jay Gould. There was a lot of talk about Astor's possible motives. Some people thought that he wanted to hurt the rival millionaires by this, and others believed that he thought a lower fare would increase travel to the Annexed District (the Bronx) where the Astors owned considerable property. It is interesting to note that no one seemed to think that he was acting to help the people riding the elevated. In any event, the bill did not pass.

William then gave his vigorous backing to a measure to remove the ugly Croton Reservoir from its location at Fifth Avenue and Forty-second Street, which was altogether too close to Astor homes and property. The bill passed the Senate, but was defeated in the Assembly.

A story went the rounds afterward that Astor made a list of all the Assemblymen who voted against his bill and that from then on he made it a point to vote against any measure they presented. This nasty tale may well be untrue, but taking the unbending character of the man into account, it is by no means improbable. Thus early in his career did a cloud of unfavorable publicity begin to hover around his head.

Driven by ambition, the following year he ran for Congress of the United States. Both Conkling and Grant made personal appearances for him, but unfortunately for Astor, the power of these men had passed its peak. William's campaign was not helped by the undeniable fact that he did not even live in the part of the city he was to represent. "I have as great an interest in the Seventh Congressional District as I have in the part of the city in which I live," he protested vainly. Unpleasant remarks were passed on his failing to campaign personally in the Avenue A district, where many of his tenements were located. Newspapers published reports that he had tried to buy votes and that he was ruled by the party machine.

William Waldorf was so enraged by this that he suggested to his father that the family as a whole move to England. John Jacob III would not hear of it and William, so domineering to others, never opposed his father.

Back in the New York State Senate after his national defeat, he had the pleasure of seeing the bill to remove the reservoir passed. It was to be his last political satisfaction. In 1881, in his bid for re-election, he came up against Roswell Pettibone Flower, a broker who was a favorite of the Tammany party machine. The *New York Times* commented gloomily on the poor caliber of both candidates and allowed that Astor was probably the lesser of the two evils. The *Sun* disagreed in a report that William Waldorf was never to forgive or forget: "Apart from his money, Mr. Astor is one of the weakest aspirants who ever stood the suffrage of a New York constituency."

Flower won in what is generally believed to have been a most corrupt election, and in time went on to become the governor of New York. As for Astor, his career as an elected representative of the people was over—but the memory lingered on, painful and embittering. His father advised: "Take the trick whenever you can and go on with the game." But proud William could not bear to lose a trick.

His political friends did not forget him, though. In 1881 President James Garfield was assassinated and Vice-President Chester A. Arthur, a longtime friend of Roscoe Conkling, succeeded him. Astor was appointed Minister to Italy. His father, John Jacob III, had found his greatest happiness in Army service in the Civil War; William Waldorf found his in Rome. Both as an Astor and as the representative of his government, William Waldorf was welcomed by King Humbert and his Queen Margherita and accepted in the highest circles. This was his first taste of how the European aristocracy lives and it was to have a profound effect on him. Even shy Mamie flowered in the kindly warmth and for the first time in her life found herself a notable hostess. She quickly became a favorite at court. When a visiting nobleman one day asked Margherita about her, the queen replied warmly: "Mrs. Astor is the most beautiful woman in Italy."

Impressed by the art treasures around him, William Waldorf began what was to become a magnificent collection, with some paintings by Holbein, Clouet, and Murillo. Like thousands of other visitors to Italy, he was enchanted with the famous Villa Borghese known the world over for its beauty. "How much would it cost to buy the entire balustrade?" he asked coolly. "Including fountains and statuary?" returned the stunned Italian owner. "Of course." A price was agreed on and it was his.

The life of a diplomat and art collector did not occupy all his time and Astor, ever restless, decided to try his hand at writing an historical romance. This novel, *Valentino,* is awkward in construction and unnatural in dialogue, yet it does have a wildly imaginative style.

The happy years in Italy came to an end when Grover Cleveland succeeded Arthur to the Presidency. In 1885 William found himself with no choice but to go back to work in the Astor Estate office. He considered the world of business unworthy of a gentleman and spent as little time there as possible.

Feeling wistful about Italy, he wrote the novel, *Sforza, a Story of Milan.* The heroine of this romantic tale masquerades as a boy and is so successful in her disguise that neither the hero nor the reader suspects her sex until she is unmasked on page 256.

The book is dedicated to "my dear wife," a small tribute to an unhappy woman doing her very best to please her difficult husband. During those years, she became the mother of two boys—need one ask their names? —William Waldorf, Jr., later known simply as Waldorf, and John Jacob Astor V, and two daughters, Pauline and Gwendolyn. Although largely absorbed in her children, Mary was not totally uninterested in leading the high society life of the period. Still, there is no question that William's insistence that Mary become *the* Mrs. Astor was for him rather than her. The extreme importance he placed on outranking his aunt must be explained by the man's boredom. He simply could not find enough to do and silly and important things became equal in his mind.

Nothing seemed to go as he would have wished it. Socially he was defeated by Caroline. His political and diplomatic careers were over. Any pleasure he might have gotten from the highly profitable real estate was spoiled for him by a steadily mounting wave of public criticism. Where his grandfather, William Backhouse Astor, landlord of New York and builder of tenements, paid no attention to any hostile remarks, William was cut to the quick.

In response to the outcry against conditions in the tenements, the mayor once again appointed an investigating committee. And once again a place for an Astor was found on the committee. The newspapers were highly critical. Convinced that he was capable of being impartial, William was amazed that anyone could object to his serving. Possibly influenced by this, he did sell about a million dollars' worth of the worst tenements.

In 1890, Jacob Riis, a journalist and social reformer, published the most slashing attack of all on the tenements, entitled, "How the Other Half Lives." Riis did not lash out at the Astors in particular. Oddly enough, he mentioned the name only once and then it was to praise William's mother, Mrs. John Jacob Astor III, for charities performed during "her noble and useful life." Still, Riis's book had a great effect and it was becoming increasingly uncomfortable to be a tenement-house owner.

It was at just this time that William's father died and William became the richest man in America. That he was richer by far than his uncle, *the* Mrs. Astor's husband William, or his cousin, John Jacob IV, was a result of his grandfather's will which left the most valuable real estate to his father. The Astors have always been secretive, and so no one has ever been sure of the exact amount of the fortune. Estimates have been made of the rent receipts. William Waldorf got a lion's share of from six to nine million dollars a year in rents from his real-estate property, and John got slightly more than three million dollars. This was a regular annual income, and it was all theirs to keep in the days before income taxes.

Showing the touch of sentimentality that was a basic

part of his nature, William kept his father's desk exactly as it had been on the last day of use. A vase of fresh roses was refilled each day on William's orders. He did not really wish to take his father's place at that desk in the small back room that the heads of the Astor family traditionally used as their office. Business, even when it was his own, continued to bore him. What is more, John Jacob Astor IV, who was sixteen years younger than he, was by then working in the office. William simply could not stand his cousin. And so he turned over the management of the Estate to others.

Even aside from business, the responsibilities that went with being head of the Astor family held little appeal for him. Although, like most Astors, John Jacob III had not been particularly charitable, he served the Astor Library as trustee and treasurer for more than thirty years and left it four hundred thousand dollars in his will. When John died, the board of the libary hopefully asked William to act as trustee in turn. Libraries for the public held no appeal at all for him and he was, if anything, annoyed by the suggestion.

The newspapers again found fault with Astor, which only irritated him further. A few years later when he was asked to approve a merger of the Astor Library with the Tilden and Lenox Libraries, he gave his approval in a quarrelsome letter: "For many years that institution (the Astor Library) has been censured by the American press sometimes along comprehensible and occasionally upon unintelligent grounds. One particular of these complaints always remains the same—that it was an appendage of the Astor family which controlled it for purposes of self-glorification to the detriment of public interest."

The attacks on his position in regard to the library and real estate made him increasingly dissatisfied with life. In the summer of 1890 he reported receiving threats that his children would be kidnapped. This was, he announced, the last straw, and he determined to quit this country forever and go to England. His estate could be handled by a distant relative, Charles A. Peabody, Jr.

There was just one loose end, his mansion on Thirty-third Street and Fifth Avenue. He decided that the best thing he could do would be to tear it down and build "the largest, most elegant hotel in the world" in its place. His great-grandfather, John Jacob I, had made a lot of money with his Astor House and his example was still being followed three generations later, even by so rebellious a personality as William Waldorf. The fact that the hotel would bother his aunt and cousin who lived next door only increased his delight in the idea. *The* Mrs. Astor snapped that she would not visit William on her trips to London, a threat which did not trouble him at all.

Before leaving for England, the newspapers quoted William as saying: "America is not a fit place for a gentleman to live."

This statement has never been forgotten and is considered rather a curse by William's English descendants, who insist that it is not true and was made up by a newspaper reporter.

William Waldorf Astor

True or false, his public image in America was ruined and the newspapers wrote of his activities in England in the most unkind style. To get back at them, in July of 1892 William had a report of his death sent to the American newspapers. Except for the *Herald,* which wisely waited for word from its London correspondent, the major papers carried obituaries. If William Waldorf had been indulging in the fantasy, "They'll be sorry when I'm dead," the news stories must have come as a terrible disappointment. Said the *New York Tribune:* "The death of William Waldorf Astor, though not an event of great and lasting significance either in the world of action or the world of thought, will be generally deplored."

William put this failure behind him and began to work his way into British high society. He soon decided that he could not possibly be accepted as *the* Mr. Astor in England unless he were Lord Astor . . . Baron Astor . . . Viscount Astor. To smooth his way, he looked for aristocratic ancestors in the hazy background of John Jacob Astor I. He hired an expert to trace and draw up a family tree that would suit him. According to this, John Jacob Astor was descended from one Jean Jacques d'Astorg, a Huguenot, who had fled to Walldorf from persecution in France in the 1680's. D'Astorg's ancestors were traced back for five hundred years to Pedro d'Astorga, who had gotten his original title from the Queen of Spain toward the end of the twelfth century. But the newspapers, at least in America, remained unconvinced. The New York *Sun* went so far as to employ an expert of its own to prove that William's family tree was just made up.

The American part of William Waldorf's life was really over. From then to the end of his life, he was to return to America only for occasional visits. He remained an absentee landlord and hotel-owner, using the wealth earned in America to obtain the position he so desperately wanted in England. A sum, reported to be one-and-a-quarter million dollars, bought him Cliveden, a magnificent country estate with a romantic history that could be traced back to 1666 when it belonged to the second Duke of Buckinghamshire. Cliveden, William decided, was destined to be the ancestral seat for generations of lordly Astors, born and unborn. To discourage curious people from coming to stare at him, he surrounded as much of the estate as possible with a wall and, it was said, had broken glass put on top.

For all his eagerness to be Lord Astor, he was not British enough to understand that the aristocrats felt a sense of responsibility to the people on their land and in the nearby villages. No one in a small town in the United States ever looked on the wealthy owner of the largest nearby estate as a protector. But in England, particularly before World War I, a modern version of feudalism had appeared in places where there was a lord who felt that the townspeople were his people and the village was his village. The tremendous difference between rich and poor in both countries—in the late nineteenth and early twentieth centuries—was accepted by most as a fact of life in England as it never was in the

United States. The wealthiest of the landed Englishmen had incomes of as much as five thousand dollars a day, while vast numbers of working men drew five dollars a week, and both groups thought this would never change.

The lord and lady of the manor were expected to take an important part in the village life, holding flower shows, attending church functions, judging Morris Dance competitions, caring for the sick and poor. It was not in Astor's character to do any of this, but it all came naturally—thanks to his providing them with the means —to the next generation.

For William Waldorf, both city and country homes were to be used to entertain as many of the right people as possible. As he still longed to be a power in the political life of a nation, he bought an influential newspaper, the *Pall Mall Gazette.* Its policy had been liberal; no matter; Astor could impose his will on it and he did. Henceforth it was to be Conservative and, as he put it, a paper "by gentlemen for gentlemen." He bought a second newspaper, the *Pall Mall Budget,* and then wishing a place to publish his own articles and stories, founded the *Pall Mall Magazine.* It also featured stories by Rudyard Kipling, James Barrie, and H. G. Wells.

The literary magazine brought William the most pleasure, but it was the newspaper that gave him hopes of rising to the British nobility. Could such a position then be bought? The British, of course, denied it, but Americans were not so sure.

"Are we to argue from Mr. Astor's apparent migration that the opportunity of the very rich lingers in

England?" asked *Harper's Weekly*. "In England they take their millionaires more seriously than we do and are much readier to give them a chance and fit them out with a suitable rank and proper employment."

But though William was happy in England, his wife was homesick for America. When she died in 1894, William yielded to her wish when it could no longer matter to her, and sent her body home to America for burial. With the same touch of sentiment that led him to keep roses on his father's desk in an office he hardly ever saw, he ordered that a blanket of fresh lilies of the valley cover her grave for years to come. He may not have loved her, but he felt her loss. Though he outlived her by quarter of a century, he never married again.

Without Mary's gently restraining hand, William became increasingly moody. He built a house on the Victoria Embankment to serve both as home and Astor Estate office, and was so afraid of being murdered that he worked out a system whereby he could, if startled by an unexpected sound, touch an invisible spring and fasten every door in every room in the house. The ground-floor windows were kept heavily barred and there was only one outside door. Not secure in this security, William Waldorf kept two revolvers, which he was quite capable of using, by his bed.

His fears seemed funny to most people then. It was a period when psychological interpretation of difficult personalities was uncommon. The fear was in fact tragic for him. "I die many deaths every day," he admitted in one of the rare moments when he revealed himself to another.

Despite these terrors, he loved England, and in 1899 decided that the moment had come for him to be an Englishman in fact as well as heart and mind, and he became a citizen.

This annoyed his former countrymen. William was quoted, possibly inaccurately: "America is good enough for any man who has to make a livelihood, though why traveled people of independent means should remain there more than a week is not readily to be comprehended."

William Waldorf was told that an effigy labeled "Astor the Traitor" had been burned in Times Square. Responding to this with the worst possible taste, he bought the flags of the United States frigate *Chesapeake,* captured by the British in the War of 1812, and presented them as a gift to the Royal United Service Museum.

This may have been the reason for a snub he received on one of his few visits to the United States. He had invited Theodore Roosevelt to dinner and Roosevelt first accepted and then sent his regrets. The story given out was that Roosevelt had believed that the Astor invitation came from John Jacob IV and his refusal came when he learned it was from William Waldorf.

William brushed off the insult and went on to conduct the main business of his visit—a check of the real estate and hotel. The Waldorf was too large and noisy a place for him to use during his rare visits. For that matter, he questioned if it were really suitable for any gentleman. He, therefore, had the Netherlands Hotel built for those too refined for the Waldorf.

In England he purchased Hever Castle, built in the thirteenth century and bought by the Boleyn family in the 1500's. Doomed young Anne Boleyn had lived there before her marriage to King Henry VIII. But she was not to be queen for long. Henry had her executed and married again . . . and again. Anne's father, avoided by his fearful neighbors, remained at Hever until his death. Henry VIII then took it over and gave it as a present to ugly Anne of Cleves, the fourth wife whom he was divorcing. The castle later passed from hand to hand until Astor appeared with ten million dollars to buy the castle, fill it with works of art, and create gardens and a lake around it.

William Waldorf was something of a mystic and he wondered whether the unquiet spirit of Anne Boleyn remained in the home from which she had gone to her marriage and death. Members of the Psychical Research Society were called in to watch for Anne each night during Christmas week, when Astor felt she was most likely to appear. But to his disappointment, she was never observed.

Although he loved Hever, most of his entertaining was done at Cliveden. A weekend at Cliveden was not always a joy for the guest. The meals were superb, as Astor loved good food, and plenty of it. He ate artichokes and shrimp as a prebreakfast snack. Still, a visit does not consist of food alone. A careful schedule was worked out by the host, with just so many hours for eating, horseback riding, walking, driving, resting, dressing, and dancing. One lady dared to stroll out in the garden at letter-writing time. After a few moments she noticed that she was being followed by a nervous servant. He approached her timidly and asked if she had perhaps forgotten that this was letter-writing time. Mr. Astor would be annoyed were he to look out and see that she was not following the schedule. Hardly able to believe her ears, she said she would leave rather than remain in any place where she could not do as she liked. Please to call her carriage. The footman, red in the face, stammered that he would not dare to call for a carriage before the time appointed by his employer for leaving.

William Waldorf was just as rigid with his children. Should one of them be a minute late to dinner, William would fix him with what the family described as a "cold and fishlike stare." This was his reaction to any other behavior that annoyed him, too. It was all a bit hard on his motherless children. The eldest boy, Waldorf, would sometimes argue with his father. Astor would listen in silence without ever changing expression. "Thank you," he would say, and make no further comment.

Hard as he may have been to live with, Astor did want to do the right thing for his children, and when his daughter Pauline came of age he decided that she must make a proper debut. Having no confidence in any female relative or friend, he felt that he could handle the affair just as well as his aunt, *the* Mrs. Astor, in America would have done. With male logic he came straight to the point: A debut was intended to introduce a girl to eligible young men, was it not? And so he wrote to the secretary of the Bachelors' Club and asked for a list of fifty bachelors to invite. Pauline managed to survive the embarrassment of this and in time married Lieutenant Colonel Herbert Henry Spender-Clay, graduate of Eton and Sandhurst and holder of the medal with six clasps for the Boer War. Her father did not live to see how close this marriage was to bring the family to the throne. Pauline's daughter Rachel grew up to marry the Honorable David Bowes-Lyon, youngest son of the Earl of Strathmore and Kinghorne, and brother to the lady who is now Queen Mother Elizabeth.

The most spectacular of the Astor marriages, however, was made by Pauline's older brother Waldorf to Nancy Langhorne Shaw of Virginia. Like the true Englishman he had become, the groom's father gave them the ancestral home, Cliveden. He had owned it, after all, for thirteen years by then. Although he still had Hever and two London houses, he was always looking for something new and spent a million dollars on a villa in Sorrento, Italy, for use during the winter months.

William could well afford such expenses by then. He had shifted some of his investments to England, but much of his fortune still came from the land and buildings of Manhattan. With the Waldorf and Netherlands hotels operating at a profit, William put eight million dollars into building the Astor Hotel on Broadway. The Astor was opened in 1904 and was an immediate success.

Its grand ballroom, capable of seating five thousand guests at one time, was constantly in use.

At one business affair, where the dinner was priced at five dollars, a guest declared in a stage whisper: "Three dollars goes for the food, one dollar to the hotel, and one dollar to the greatest absentee landlord in the world."

The guest might have been interested in learning that stores on the ground floor of the hotel brought that landlord an additional $240,000 in rent money a year.

Even though the width of an ocean separated him from the bulk of his real estate, he was quick to recognize that huge apartment houses were going to change the face of the cities of America. Under Astor's orders two tall dwellings, the Apthorp and the Belnord, were put up on land that had been bought for a few thousand dollars by William B. Astor in 1860. They stand to this day, massive and decorated with ornate stonework. In William Waldorf's time heavy wrought-iron gates would swing open to allow carriages into an inner court protected by a uniformed guard.

Successful from the start, Astor's American ventures made possible the purchase of another highly influential British newspaper, the *Sunday Observer,* founded in 1781. His determination to become a lord never weakened. Prominent politicians had learned that his heart was extremely soft when appeals for campaign fund donations were made. Collectors for British charities were not turned away with the John Jacob I retort that wealth does not increase the "disposition to do good."

And at last on King George's New Year's List in 1916 William's name appeared. On April 16, his tall figure dressed in red velvet robes trimmed with ermine, Astor heard the clerk in the House of Lords announce the appointment of "our trusty cousin, William Waldorf Astor to . . . Baron Astor of Hever Castle."

A magnificent coat of arms was designed for the new lord with "a falcon resting on a dexter hand couped at the wrist . . . in chief two fleurs-de-lis . . ." and in remembrance of John Jacob Astor I, "on the dexter a North American Indian and on the sinister, a North American Fur Trapper."

"There does not seem to be much enthusiasm displayed in English papers on the new peer's behalf," wrote the *Literary Digest*.

But what cared Astor? The opinions of others meant nothing to him. He had what he wanted, and there was more to come. In June of the following year in the King's Birthday Honors, he was made a Viscount. This title is more important than the barony. William had achieved his life's ambition and he had secured his family's position in the British nobility. Although a younger son cannot inherit his father's title, years later John Jacob Astor V won the barony for himself in reward "for public services."

No one could have been more British than this branch of the Astor family was to become. Their money came from America, but their role in American history was at an end. Fewer than forty years later William's grandson, the Honorable Michael Astor, was to write:

William Waldorf Astor

"Although I enormously enjoy my visits to the United States, while I am there, I can never escape the feeling of being in a completely foreign country."

His children became prominent in British politics, but William did not. He could have sat in the House of Lords, but as often happens, the opportunity to take a part in public life came when he no longer wanted it. Astor appeared in the House of Lords only on each of the two occasions when he was granted a title.

The last two years of his life were an anticlimax, ending in a manner as far removed from the noble as could be imagined. On October 18, 1919, he went into the bathroom after a dinner of roast mutton and macaroni, and did not reappear. When at last his valet broke in, it was to find Baron Astor of Hever, the first Viscount Astor, dead.

6

John Jacob Astor IV,
the Richest Man on the *Titanic*

"YOU HAVE JUST SAID that Mr. Astor never sold?"

"Once in a while he sells, yes."

"Isn't it almost a saying in this community that the Astors buy and never sell?" persisted the counsel of a Senate Committee studying taxes and property valuation.

This policy originated many years earlier by John Jacob Astor I was still in force when John Jacob Astor IV took his place in the Astor Estate office. No two accounts of the period agree as to how much time John Jacob IV devoted to the family business, some reporting that he directed it personally, and others insisting that he left it to the trustees and agents. The truth probably lies somewhere between the two positions. It is clear that John was more interested in the property than his father had been and was fairly often seen behind the heavily barred windows of the two-story red brick building that housed the Astor Estate office on Twenty-sixth Street.

He can have felt nothing but profound relief when his unpleasant cousin, William Waldorf Astor, packed up and took off for England. The Astor Estate offices remained partitioned, with one-half occupied by the seven clerks and managers running William Waldorf's half of the real estate, while the other housed John when he was there, his three managers when they were there, and twenty-two clerks who were always there.

John Jacob IV moved into a modest office that was in striking contrast to the grandeur of his home. He sat behind a roll-top desk, moving to a table when he needed to open his ledgers. A few plainly framed pictures and a red carpet were the only decorations. Two windows opened onto a narrow court and faced a blank wall.

Even so, the office may have come to seem a refuge to him from his home and particularly from his wife, who made his life miserable.

"Ava [pronounced Ah-vah] was the most beautiful woman I have ever seen," says an old woman who knew the couple. "It was an era of great beauties, but they all took a back seat to her. When she walked into a room every eye was on her. But she was cold, hard, selfish, and mean to her husband. I don't think she was capable of loving anyone."

Her beauty had captivated John, as it did everyone else. She was the belle of Newport each summer and Philadelphia each winter. The townspeople of Newport, who in those days lined up to watch the Casino Balls at a cost of a dollar a ticket, looked for Ava first, to see with whom she was dancing and to admire her elegance. The beauty of her face with its Roman nose and dark flashing eyes was matched by her narrow-waisted, full-bosomed figure. Those who knew her still speak warmly of the flawless back shown in her low-cut evening gowns; even her ankles, feet, and hands were of surpassing loveliness. A vain and confident girl, she was determined to bring off a brilliant marriage and John was described in the gossip columns as "one of the richest catches of the day." She overlooked, at least at first, his strangely shaped receding forehead, concentrating her attention instead on his slender, narrow-shouldered elegant figure. John was used to his dominating mother, and so he was not put off by Ava's sharp tongue. "We do not converse in Newport, we eat," she squelched him as he tried to make small talk at one of the endless dinners. He did not realize until too late that Ava was really nothing like his adoring mother.

Ava married him, but she did not feel she needed to be nice to him or to the son, William Vincent, whom she bore in the first year of their marriage. Vincent, the name by which the child was to be known, was in memory of Count von Rumpff, husband of his ancestor Eliza. Her son's clumsiness irritated Ava beyond endurance. Cursed from babyhood with huge hands and feet, Vincent was always knocking things down. His mother did not hesitate to raise her cultured voice in a shout of

"Stupid!" at him in front of a roomful of people. Her guests found this more amusing than the family did.

And there were always guests whether the family was wintering at the mansion on Fifth Avenue, summering at Beechwood in Newport, or spending between-season periods at Ferncliff, the estate William Astor had loved. Ava called in Stanford White, society's favorite architect, and had him create an athletic compound of a tennis court, two squash courts, a sixty-five-foot-long marble swimming pool, dressing rooms, a rifle range, bowling alley, and a billiard room. Ava most enjoyed tennis or bridge, while John played tennis only. A strangely revealing snapshot has somehow survived to show the prevailing spirit of those long-ago weekends. John Jacob is on the tennis court stretching his long thin arm up to serve the ball, while Ava is seated on the sidelines, her back carefully turned to the tennis game. She took to devoting more and more time at Ferncliff to bridge, an activity that John hated.

"He shambled from room to room, tall, loosely built and ungraceful, rather like a great overgrown colt, in a vain search for someone to talk to," recalled Elizabeth Lehr, who with her prankish husband, Harry Lehr, was a regular guest at the Astors.

Punctuality had been drilled into John as a boy and he saw it as a part of a proper code of behavior, but Ava could not be bothered to leave the bridge table until it was too late for her and the other players to appear at dinner on time. Sundays were perhaps the worst days for John; he would go to church alone, correct in his cutaway coat and top hat, leaving his wife and her friends at the bridge table.

In time John found ways of relieving his boredom. He wrote a science fiction novel about the future, entitled *A Journey into Other Worlds*. This is not well written, but it does show that Ava's stiff, awkward husband had a lively imagination and considerable knowledge of science and engineering. The men of the future, as Astor saw it, would learn to control the weather and make rain to order—matters that are today under serious scientific study. The Aleutian Islands would be blown up to allow the Japanese currents to warm the Arctic. Space travel is made possible by the force of "apergy," the opposite of gravity. All transportation on the face of the earth is driven by electricity, instead of the horse. War, characterized by airplane bombing, has become so terrible that the world is united. Germs are used to destroy poisonous or harmful animals. The Astor eye for profit is not completely closed either. The hero, Colonel Bearwarden, approaches the planet Jupiter with excitement: "How I should like to mine those hills for copper!" The love story is handled with far less skill than the sections dealing with science or business—true in the author's life as well as in his writing.

It was indeed fortunate for John that he was able to find outlets for his energies that did not depend on his wife. He had natural mechanical ability and was happiest working with his hands. John spent hours of his spare time on a series of inventions, including an improved bicycle brake, a system for attaching vacuum cups to the legs of steamship chairs so that they would stay in one place on a rolling deck, and a marine turbine engine. His "pneumatic road improver," capable of blowing dirt off roads, won first prize at the World's Columbian Exposition in Chicago in 1893. Astor was generous with his inventions, if with nothing else, and presented them to the public as a gift.

Considering his mechanical bent and his wealth, he was naturally one of the first men in the country to own the newly invented automobile. Even Ava was excited by this and agreed to accompany him down Fifth Avenue in a surrey with a steam-driven engine under the seat. Little Vincent, to whom his father was much attached, was taken along for the ride. Ava was used to excited comments from onlookers, and John Jacob was filled with the pride of ownership, so neither saw anything but admiration and envy in the shouts and gestures of the crowds on the sidewalk. They remained blissfully unaware of the fact that the engine had caught fire until the heat became so intense that they were forced to jump from the burning car.

This accident did not dampen John's enthusiasm and he soon became the owner of eighteen cars, among them a European racer with a seventy-horsepower engine. By 1903 he was boasting that he could drive the hundred and fifteen miles from New York to Newport in a mere four hours and twenty minutes.

Although he liked yachting nearly as much as driving, he had no natural ability as a captain and one summer's afternoon ran into the Vanderbilts' yacht. The Vanderbilts were millionaires, too, but were not prepared to pay for the repairs and sued Astor for fifteen thousand dollars in damages. He rallied from this blow to redecorate the *Nourmahal* and expanded the dining room so that it could seat sixty fearless guests. For reasons not clear to anyone else, he was extremely worried about pirates and had four guns mounted on the deck. But John Jacob had guessed wrong; no pirates attacked and the *Nourmahal* met disaster only in the form of some rocks that were clearly behaving in an aggressive way.

There was no lack of money to indulge the *Nourmahal* and his other costly tastes. However Ava may have felt about her husband's personality, she was perfectly satisfied with his bank account. In 1890 the combined fortune of John Jacob Astor IV and William Waldorf Astor was put at a little under two hundred million dollars by Charles F. Southmayd, a lawyer for the Astor Estate.

The population and, therefore, the worth of the tenements increased steadily. "The more wretched the immigrants, the more valuable the land becomes," wrote an observer of the period, adding that a hundred people were being jammed into space that fifty years earlier had been occupied by a single family.

Astor's reputation for great wealth was such that he received between thirty and forty begging letters a day, and this was a period when most poor people could not write. One letter sent from Sweden was addressed to the

John Jacob Astor IV

"Richest Man in All the World: Honored Sir—I would like you to send me at once thirty thousand thalers; a mere bagatelle to you, but a fortune to me."

The Astors were not charitable in any event, as John Garvey, described in the newspapers of the time as the "Astor tramp," was to learn. Garvey stumbled into John Jacob's mansion one winter's night and finding an empty bed in the servants' quarters, fell asleep. When Garvey was found the following morning, Astor was in a rage. He insisted on having the tramp indicted for burglary. As Garvey was pitiful and clearly feeble-minded, Astor was vigorously attacked in the press. John was quite unable to understand why this should be. Although imaginative in some ways, he held a view of the poor that was remarkably similar to that of his grandfather, William Backhouse. Poverty was beyond his understanding.

The tramp, it is likely, had wandered into Astor's mansion drawn by the lights and activity of the hotel next door. It was just another sign, thought John, of the way a hotel, however luxurious, changes a neighborhood. William Waldorf's Hotel Waldorf had annoyed John from the stormy March night in 1893 when it opened.

William was hardly ever in New York and his cousin had to look on enviously from the sidelines at the Waldorf's success. With William away, the hotel was managed by George Boldt, who used to say: "I should prefer to see Mrs. Astor drinking an unprofitable cup of water in the Palm Garden than to serve a rich newcomer the most expensive dinner."

Dinners were overseen by Oscar Tschirsky, who was soon to lose his last name and become known simply as "Oscar of the Waldorf." Boldt checked every other detail carefully, insisting that candlesticks be placed in each room, as electricity in those days often failed. One day Boldt decided that refinement demanded the entire staff be clean shaven. All beards had to go, with a single exception, his own sleek, spade-shaped beard. He went so far as to insist that the cab drivers who stationed themselves at the Thirty-third Street entrance of the hotel shave off their beards. Waiters, cooks, porters, and handymen complained, and frantic meetings were called by the Association of Hack Drivers. Objections meant nothing to Boldt, and the beards soon disappeared.

He could afford to be arrogant. Every one of the rooms that had been reserved for permanent guests was quickly occupied. Oscar claimed that on an ordinary day twenty-five thousand people walked down the red-carpeted corridor known as Peacock Alley. Even William Waldorf walked down Peacock Alley—once; he stayed in the hotel on but a single occasion. That time he saw as little as possible. Staff members reported that he never raised his eyes from the carpet and dashed down the hall as if pursued, entered the elevator, head down, and was taken to his room.

But Boldt was not satisfied: he still wanted Mrs. Astor with her unprofitable cup of water. The question was how to get her. In those days ladies dined only in carefully selected homes, not in a public place. *The* Mrs. Astor was at last enticed into the Waldorf by an exceptionally fashionable ball. Hearing that there was a depression in the winter of 1896–97, a rich society woman, Cornelia Sherman Martin, naively observed that a costume ball for nine hundred guests would be a charitable act, because it would "give an impetus to trade." Society members did their best to oblige, and one man paid a costume-maker ten thousand dollars to create a suit of gold-inlaid armor for him to wear. *The* Mrs. Astor did not mean to go, but could not resist Harry Lehr's urging. Then, too, she was pleased that her son was selected by Mrs. Martin to be her ball partner, an honor that won him the title "King" of the ball. It is the only social occasion on record in which John shone more brightly than his wife.

The public and the press were outraged by Mrs. Martin's extravagance at a time when thousands were starving. Attacks were so violent that the Martins fled the country and went to England to live. Nonetheless, from the viewpoint of the Waldorf's managers, the ball was a huge success.

John Jacob IV was discovering that he could hardly ignore the activity and excitement of the Waldorf. His mother and he were forced to realize that home life so close to the hotel was hopeless and moved thirty blocks uptown to 840 Fifth Avenue. Everyone was asking what they planned to do with their old home. For a while Astor threatened to build a stable there. He had a rather nasty sense of humor and figured this was a sure way of infuriating his cousin. Boldt became frantic and rushed to one of the Astor Estate's business advisers, Abner Bartlett, pleading with him to do something. Bartlett had little trouble in convincing John Jacob IV to do what came naturally—make a hotel of his former home that would be even grander than the Waldorf.

All his life John competed desperately with his cousin. William Waldorf had married a beautiful woman; John then married the most beautiful woman of the era. William produced a historical novel; John wrote one about the future. Now came the Waldorf Hotel with its 450 bedrooms and 350 baths, its Empire Room that was a copy of the grand salon in King Ludwig's palace in Munich, its Palm Gardens where guests were required to wear full evening dress, and its guest list made up of royalty, diplomats, socialites, and celebrities in the arts and politics. John Jacob IV set out to create an even better hotel of his own. Still, he could not be completely independent, as his house was next door to the Waldorf and logically had to be connected. John did have his little triumph over William, because the Astoria was made taller than the Waldorf and cast a shadow on the older hotel.

As, like all of her children, John was devoted to his mother, he wanted to name the hotel the Schermerhorn, which was her maiden name. That was too much for William Waldorf to endure, as he hated *the* Mrs. Astor. A compromise was worked out and the second hotel was named Astoria in memory of the fur empire of John Jacob Astor I. Ward McAllister's daughter Louise suggested brightly that the names be combined and hy-phenated, and she and her friends used to say "meet me at the hyphen." Linked by more than a hyphen, the combined hotel flourished as no hotel had ever flour-ished before.

As it is human nature not to value what one has, As-tor took his profitable hotel and his tremendous real-estate holdings for granted and longed instead for a military career. He was influenced no doubt by his uncle's romantic reminiscences of the Civil War and his father's regrets at not having been allowed to serve. In 1895 John joined the military staff of New York's Gov-ernor Levi P. Morton, but peacetime military service is nothing very much to satisfy a bored millionaire.

Three years later the Americans became involved in the Cuban effort to win independence from Spain. The incident that was to bring this country into war took place on February 15, 1898, when the battleship *Maine* was blown up in Havana harbor and 260 men were killed. The explosion was believed to have been caused by a mine set in the harbor. The public naturally as-sumed the Spanish were to blame, and war between Spain and the United States was declared.

John Jacob rushed to offer both his yacht and him-self to the government. He had the daring idea of pre-senting an entire battery of artillery. The government accepted and Peyton C. March, who later became a gen-eral, was sent by the Army to New York to take com-mand. But when he arrived, he could not find any trace of the soldiers. He went to the Astor Estate office where he was told with a smile that the "Astor Light Battery is simply a checkbook." But a checkbook has power, and men were quickly recruited and drilled on Astor land in the Bronx. Both March and Astor tried to get educated men for their brigade. They were delighted when the captain of the Cornell University football team signed up.

Uniforms were made to measure in four days, with the tailors receiving a bonus for working so fast. A second set of tropical uniforms was then added, as it appeared that the battery might be sent to the Philippine Islands, which were also fighting against the Spanish rulers. Astor then heard that some excellent guns were to be had in France and he sent a cable ordering them. He learned only then that Spanish destroyers would stop any ships carrying arms to America. An elaborate plan was worked out, and the guns were first smuggled into Belgium and then brought over the ocean hidden in a coal bunker on a merchant ship. At this point Astor discovered that the Army had no manual explaining the use of such guns, and so he had one written and printed.

The battery was sent to the Philippines where it took part in the attack on Manila. Two of the men were killed and eight were wounded. The surviving soldiers were permitted to keep their uniforms, and the Army received the guns and ammunition.

John Jacob was not content to sit out the war and let his battery do all the fighting. His influential friends arranged for him to meet Theodore Roosevelt, who was then Assistant Secretary of the Navy. With Roosevelt's assistance he was appointed inspector general with the rank of lieutenant colonel. Astor inspected army camps in the United States, and then his wish was granted and he was sent to Cuba. He was present at the decisive battle of Santiago until the victory after a week of bitter fighting. Unfortunately for his military ambitions, he caught malaria and this cut short his army career. It was a brief war, in any event, and he had done enough to be promoted to colonel for "faithful and meritorious service" and he enjoyed hearing that title for the rest of his life.

Astor returned home to his lovely but cold wife, to his warm but aging mother, to the temperamental little son he loved, and to the Astor Estate. Although he was director of some companies, trustee and large stockholder in others, he was never involved in running them. Throughout his life the real estate was the only business in which he took a personal interest.

On October 27, 1904, an event took place that was to increase the values of all New York City real estate in general and Astor land in particular. Handsome Mayor George B. McClellan, son of John Jacob Astor III's favorite general, turned the sterling silver handle of the throttle of the city's first subway, and the train left City Hall Station, ran along under Fourth Avenue to Grand Central Station, then west to Times Square and up Broadway until it finally reached its northernmost point at 145th Street. During the course of that historic afternoon, the Astors and fifteen thousand other important personages took their first subway rides by invitation. The subway was opened to an eager and excited public that evening and the first rush hour was underway. "Men fought, kicked and pummeled one another in their mad desire to ride on the trains," reported the New York *World*. "Women were dragged out, either screaming in hysterics, or in a swooning condition."

The Astors, who had vigorously fought the coming of the subway for two generations, had no need to swoon or scream. Every piece of mid-town property overnight became more valuable. As the subway grew, mile by mile, the Astor fortune grew with it. Once again, as had happened in the great days of John Jacob I and William Backhouse, the Astors could sit back and let the city work for them. The subway was extended to the Bronx; the route selected went right through Astor land, a fact hardly surprising to anyone aware of the family's influence with politicians. What is more, the Astors insisted on being paid for allowing the subway to pass through their property. Offered $12,000 for a right of way, John Jacob IV insisted on $129,000 and got it.

Although he was always slow to accept change, he grasped what the development of steel construction would do for buildings. Skyscrapers, twenty or twenty-five stories high, a truly magnificent source of income, could be erected. Astor was quick to invest in both apartment houses and commercial buildings. A single office building, the Schermerhorn, brought in $75,000 in rent a year from the American Surety Company. Even then, the Astor tenements remained as a major source of rents and of misery. John Jacob IV received $4,260 in rent from the sublandlord of a single twenty-five-foot lot.

The sweatshops continued to prosper, despite the many attacks on them and opposition from the first labor unions. A New York City law in 1889 had actually prohibited the manufacture of tobacco in a tenement, but it was later declared unconstitutional. Astor himself, his friends declared, knew very little about the conditions in the tenements built by the sublandlords. He may even have been unaware that forty years after the passage of fireproofing laws, many of his tenements were fire traps, lacking fire escapes. A sublandlord could put up an unsafe tenement for $17,812, while it would cost him $20,342 to build one with moderate (not the best) safety measures. Any fire resulted in tremendous losses of lives, as by the early 1900's five hundred families were packed in the single Astor-owned block at Avenue A and First Avenue.

At about this time John Jacob decided to get rid of some of the worst of the old tenements put up by William B. Astor. He sold fifty tenements in the First Avenue district for $850,000, more than the value of the land alone. The Astors, it can be seen, had not lost their ability to bargain.

Ready for a new interest in life, John had two new hotels built—the Knickerbocker and the St. Regis. Of all his hotels, the St. Regis became the one that was closest to John's heart, an enthusiasm he passed on to his son Vincent. He applied his mechanical gifts to its construction and designed a system of heating and air conditioning, notable for the period in that each guest was able to control the temperature of his own room.

His successes with his hotels and real estate did not make up for his unhappiness at home. The birth of a daughter, Alice Muriel, did not provide a lasting reconciliation. Astor accompanied Ava to all major society events, but it was clear that he would have preferred to be alone and that she would have preferred to be with someone else. A breakup of their marriage was clearly coming, but they put it off, as John could not bear to hurt his mother, who was ill. And then in 1908 *the* Mrs. Astor died, and the divorce proceedings got underway.

The divorce became final in 1910. Astor received the news while cruising on the *Nourmahal* with Vincent, a boy of eighteen and his father's favorite companion. John returned to New York and gave a party for a hundred and fifty guests, spending twenty-five thousand dollars for flowers, decorations, favors, food, wines, and music.

It was not long before he fell in love, this time with a girl completely different from his first wife. As to age, Madeleine Talmadge Force might have been Ava's daughter; she was slightly younger than Vincent Astor. In appearance she was blonde and slender, pretty rather than beautiful, appealing rather than queenly. In character she was uncertain rather than domineering, and in emotions she was passionate rather than cold.

Astor's friends refused to take the romance seriously until the September day in 1911 when he landed his yacht at Newport, handed his dainty fiancée ashore, and set out in search of a minister to perform the ceremony. The wedding took place in the huge ballroom at Beech-wood, the "cottage" John had inherited from his mother. He was forty-seven years old and Madeleine was eighteen—and society frowned.

The criticism was so unpleasant that neither of them could endure it. Soon after the wedding they left New York and traveled first to Egypt and later to England. The following spring Madeleine was expecting a child and they decided to return home so that she could give birth in the United States.

At that time a new luxury liner, the *Titanic,* was preparing to make its first trip across the Atlantic. It was not only the largest ship ever built, but also the fastest, and it had many features designed to make it perfectly safe. "The *Titanic,*" the passengers were assured, "is unsinkable."

The Astors joined the many rich and famous people who made up the passenger list. The trip was particularly gay, with the women appearing in magnificent gowns for the dancing each night. During a short stop a salesman boarded the *Titanic.* On an impulse Astor bought Madeleine a lace jacket for eight hundred dollars.

The night of April 14-15, 1912, began as happily as all the others on this voyage. The *Titanic* was in the North Atlantic, south of Newfoundland. During that night some other ships sent warnings that huge icebergs were floating in the chill sea. Little attention was paid to them. The *Titanic* was trying to make a speed record, to go across the Atlantic faster than any vessel in history, and the officers did not want to reduce the speed and lose valuable time. The great liner, therefore, was traveling at full speed when at 2:20 A.M., it hit an iceberg. The passengers felt the crash, but did not realize how terrible a thing had happened. Captain Edward J. Smith saw to his horror that the safety devices gave no protection against this kind of collision. Water rushed into the ship, and it soon became clear that it was going to sink. Captain Smith hurried to tell his important passenger, Mr. Astor, of the disaster in private, before allowing the general alarm to be given. John accepted the news with his customary quiet dignity and led Madeleine up on deck.

A wild scene took place on the deck as crew and passengers discovered that the "unsinkable" ship did not carry enough lifeboats for the 2,224 people on board. Women and children were urged into the boats by the more courageous of the men. A few pushed the women aside and took their places in the lifeboats. Nothing could have been more foreign to Astor's character. He displayed calm courage in all the frenzy. Madeleine, always emotional and loving, clung to John. She wanted to stay on board and go down with him.

"Get into the lifeboat," he told her gently, "to please me."

"To please me" was an expression he had often used with her.

As the lifeboat pulled away, leaving behind her

doomed husband and hundreds of others, tender-hearted Madeleine heard a child crying from cold. She immediately took off her shawl and gave it to the little one, accepting the mother's thanks with her sweet smile.

The following morning when the news reached a stunned world, readers of the New York *American* were given the distinct impression that the tragedy lay in the loss of John Jacob Astor IV. The lead of the story was given over to an account of his career and history. At the bottom, as a sort of afterthought, came the mention of the fifteen hundred other men and women who had also been lost on the *Titanic*.

7

Nancy Astor,
an American Woman in Parliament

THE MOST OVERPOWERING personality the English Astor family ever had was neither English nor an Astor. She was Nancy Witcher Langhorne Shaw of Virginia, who married Waldorf Astor, eldest son of William Waldorf. Nancy's influence on British politics was great—sometimes for good, and sometimes not. Still, there is no question that she did much to improve the position of women.

"My mother had two strains in her character," said her eldest son, the late Lord William Astor, "a worldly and wild strain which came from her father and a deeply religious one. Both could be seen in her throughout her life."

Nancy, one of eleven children, had a pleasant childhood, not much occupied with education. This sketchy schooling was to prove a major handicap to Nancy, whose career was to make demands on her that she was not prepared to meet. Still, she had read the Bible from cover to cover by the time she was fourteen, impressed by a six-foot-three-inch tall parson from Kent doing missionary work in America. This, she always maintained, made up for her other educational failings.

From girlhood on, she became accustomed to being known as one of the "five beautiful Langhorne sisters" —not as the most beautiful, however. The great beauty of the family was her older sister, Irene, who married artist Charles Dana Gibson and served as model for his Gibson Girl pictures. Nancy had a kind of bright, lively good looks. Her features were clean cut and aquiline, her blue-gray eyes were always dancing, and her figure was small and trim, brisk in its movements.

When very young, Nancy was married to Robert Gould Shaw II, son of a famous abolitionist who had died leading a Negro regiment in the Civil War. The marriage was unhappy from the start. Shaw was a heavy drinker, and for the rest of her life Nancy was to hate liquor and refuse to have it served in her home. A child, Robert, was born, but nothing could save the marriage.

Nancy divorced Shaw in 1903 after six tragic years and went to England with little Robert to meet some new people. Her personality was both challenging and appealing. A society matron greeted her with the words: "I suppose you've come over to England to take one of our husbands away from us." Nancy snapped right back: "If you knew what difficulty I had getting rid of my first one, you wouldn't say that."

THE ASTORS

As the Astors were prominent in London society Nancy soon came in contact with them. The first Astor whom she met was the one she was least able to get along with—Ava, who spent much time in England to get away from her own unhappy marriage with John Jacob IV. The two women were alike in their desire to charm, startle, and shock those around them, and both had the ability to take the center of the stage. If one must compare weapons, Ava was the more beautiful, and Nancy the wittier.

Her second Astor was the man she married, who by coincidence had been born on the same day as she, May 19, 1879. Completely different in character from her ex-husband, Waldorf Astor was quiet, reserved, serious, responsible, and conscientious, a man whom Nancy could admire. He was neither handsome nor homely, with his big nose, large brown eyes, dark mustache, and curly hair. His tall thin figure had the elegance that was characteristic of the Astor men.

Waldorf spent weeks worrying how to tell his unreasonable father about his love for an American divorcée. Unpredictable William Waldorf took the news with calm: "If she's good enough for you, Waldorf, she's good enough for me."

And indeed, with Nancy as mistress, Cliveden fulfilled every one of William Waldorf's ambitions for it. One would have to look far to find a more perfect example of the great landed estates in the years before World War I. Forty gardeners tended the gardens, parks, and fruit and vegetable farms. Nancy ran the house with the help of twenty indoor servants—eight housemaids plus four kitchen maids, a groom of the chambers, an odd-job man, a chef, valet, butler, and three footmen. Until World War I the last four named powdered their hair and wore knee breeches. The stables of racehorses, under Waldorf's supervision, became among the finest in England. Cliveden was the center of the world for everyone who lived there, worked in the house or grounds, or cared for White Place, the Farm. One building on the estate was a social club containing a billiard room and a hall with a stage for performances. A fancy-dress ball for all employes was held there each winter. On Saturdays cricket or football matches were played against teams similarly made up of people living or working on the neighboring estates.

Cliveden was a social center, too, and its forty-six bedrooms were usually filled for the weekends. The guests found Nancy's gaiety contagious, though they never could tell whether she was joking or being serious. At dinner she liked to startle people by popping a huge set of celluloid false teeth into her mouth and going right on talking without a break. Turning on a southern dialect, she would hold the table enthralled with her stories about the Negroes of her native Virginia. If she were in the mood to perform more elaborately, she would invite her guests into the library after dinner, arrange the chairs as in a theater and begin to act. She might be a refined lady of incredibly good breeding who thought Americans were common or a perfectly horrible old shrew with no teeth and dark suspicions of everyone. Sometimes the other guests, inspired by her example, would join in. Her husband never did, being solemn and dignified.

Waldorf's quiet ways may have been the result of the ill health that troubled him throughout his life. His heart was weak and at the age of twenty-six, he had been stricken with tuberculosis. Even so, he decided to go into politics and in 1910 was elected to the House of Commons as the Conservative representative of Plymouth. He was a good M.P. (Member of Parliament) and was re-elected several times thereafter.

The Astors had by then become the parents of William Waldorf, born in 1907, and (Nancy) Phyllis Louise in 1909. Three years later there was another son, (Francis) David Langhorne. Child-bearing turned Nancy into a semi-invalid. Her doctors ordered a rest cure and she spent much of each day in bed. But Nancy had a restless nature and was perfectly miserable. Her health showed no improvement until in 1913 she learned about Christian Science, a religion based on the belief that love, prayer, and faith in God's goodness will conquer both evil and illness. Strengthened by this religion, she rose from her bed. She liked to say that from the day she became a Christian Scientist she was never tired or ill again.

The following year World War I broke out and Nancy and Waldorf had the tennis court building at Cliveden turned into a two-hundred-bed hospital for Canadian soldiers. The patients were constantly being startled by Nancy. On entering the hospital one day, she overheard a nurse saying that two soldiers who had been severely burned had lost the will to live. Nancy bent over them: "You're going to die and I would, too, rather than go back to Canada." They instantly defended their country against this insult and by the time she was through with them, they both wanted to live. "You have to insult men to rouse them up," she remarked airily to the stunned nursing staff. She interrupted her visits only briefly for the birth of Michael in 1916 and John Jacob VII in 1918.

Waldorf's health had been too poor for him to serve in the army in World War I. The closest he came to it was as an inspector in the quartermaster corps with the rank of major. His brother, John Jacob Astor V, had an outstanding military career, winning the French Legion of Honor, and losing a leg in battle. Waldorf remained in Parliament and was named a member of several government commissions dealing with wartime medical research.

In 1919 his father died and Waldorf inherited the title of Viscount Astor. It was a title which he really did not want and which he could not give up. As a lord, he would not be allowed to remain in the House of Commons, but would have to move to the all but powerless House of Lords. "Some people find it hard to get titles," murmured Nancy; "Lord Astor is finding it even harder to get rid of his."

Hope of saving his political career did not die all at once; he introduced a bill to allow lords to be elected to Commons. He never imagined that such a bill would not be passed until 1963. His main worry was that another man would be elected in his place. It was hardly likely, thought Astor, that this man would later step aside in his favor. It was then that he had a brainstorm —why not have his wife become a candidate for his seat in Commons. She would hold the office for him until he could take it back. Women had been given the vote and the right to sit in Commons in 1918, although no one had done so.

The candidacy of inexperienced Lady Astor startled England and America. "Will she win on popularity?" asked the London *Times*. Of course she would, and did, by a majority of three thousand votes. She liked to point out that she was physically responsible for one of them. On election day in Plymouth she heard a woman holding a baby complain loudly: "I can't vote, as I have no one to leave the baby with!" Nancy took the infant and the woman went to vote.

On December 2, 1919, Lady Astor became the first woman to be seated in the House of Commons. (She was not the first woman elected. That honor went to Constance, Countess Markievicz, who belonged to the Irish Revolutionary movement and hated the English. In order to show her contempt for them, she refused to take her seat.)

"Parliament was like a men's club," Nancy said later. "No one wanted me there."

Never one to stay in the background, she practised

her golf swing on the terrace of the House during the tea break. The public and the newspapers loved her.

"I have been in it (Commons) a week, and I never saw a house where women were more needed." She told one audience of women: "Don't blame men. They are just what we have made them and the mistake we have made is to tell them that they are the stronger sex, knowing in our hearts that they are not. They are the nicer sex, but not the stronger."

Nancy quickly settled down to fighting for the things she believed in—an end to drunkenness, and most important, improvement of the position of women.

"We are not asking for superiority, for we have always had that," she declared to the delight of all female listeners. "All we ask is equality."

Everybody paid attention to Lady Astor. Her influence was tremendous and she did a great deal to raise women from what was then second place status.

Her breezy, confident manner infuriated the late Winston Churchill, who was to be prime minister in World War II. His attitude angered her, too. "If I were your wife I'd put poison in your coffee," she burst out one day. And he replied coolly: "And if I were your husband I'd drink it."

But neither Winston Churchill nor anyone else could intimidate her. "I am always a nuisance," she remarked. "You have to be if you have strong convictions."

On a trip to the United States in the early 1920's she was asked not to discuss the League of Nations, which preceded the United Nations. After World War I the

Americans had refused to join the League and there was a great deal of bad feeling. Nancy talked about the League, disposing of the objections by saying that she had been told not to mention the League of Nations, so she would call it the "League of Peace."

She looked in on the Astor Estate office in New York one day and remarked: "It is bad business to tolerate slums." Then Nancy pointed out that bad housing ruins the health of its tenants. Somehow she appeared unaware that a part of her husband's wealth came from his American slum property.

In England, too, she favored better housing, answering those who said she was too rich to know what she was talking about: "One did not need to be born in a slum to have a heart."

Those were Lady Astor's great years in public life and everyone loved "Our Nancy," as she was called. Campaigning was a positive delight to her. She would appear on the street or in a courtyard in Plymouth and shout: "Hey, you there!" Heads would bob out of windows and she would begin to speak. She responded to hecklers with the jokes that were known as "Astorisms."

"Come on, I'm ready for you," she would cry and she was.

"You have enough brass to make a kettle," yelled one.

"You have enough water in your head to fill it," she returned.

A farmer wanting to show that she was ignorant of farm matters cried: "How many toes are there on a pig's foot?"

"Take off your shoe, man, and count for yourself."

A woman in the crowd rushed for Nancy to kiss her baby. The infant, frightened by the noise, was crying, but when Lady Astor picked him up, he began to play with her necklace and quieted down: "The way to keep children happy," she remarked cheerfully, "is to let them play with a rope of pearls."

"Your husband's a millionaire, ain't he?" asked an unfriendly workman.

Waldorf Astor, who was standing there, looked pained, but Nancy replied cheerfully: "That's one of the reasons I married him. And don't you wish you were rich?"

Astor had accepted the fact that his own political career was over, and did all he could to help hers. As the London *Times* put it: "The limelight fell almost exclusively on her, but her husband's judgment and public spirit were always of much influence behind the political scene."

Everyone who knew Waldorf speaks of his fair-minded attitude, greatness of spirit, and upright character. A brother-in-law goes so far as to describe him as a saint. But his goodness was such as to make him a remote personality. He lacked understanding of others less perfect than he. His standards for his children were almost impossible for them to live up to.

One of his few peculiarities was a fear of tuberculosis, natural enough as he had suffered it, but in his case touched with a degree of hysteria. When he traveled with the children, for example, a cow from the Cliveden farm went right along on the train, together with a farmer to milk it. How else, he asked, could one be certain that the children might not drink milk from a tubercular cow? His fear, to be fair, did have some scientific basis, as Waldorf had considerable knowledge of animal care and farming. He wrote a number of books on scientific agriculture. Yet, for all his theoretical knowledge, he never tried to run the farm at Cliveden.

He was similarly distant in his handling of the enormous estate that was supporting him and his family, leaving it to his managers. The British portion of the Astor Estate at that time consisted of about fifty million dollars in American real estate left to him by his father, and thousands of shares of stocks and bonds.

Living in England on money earned in America meant that Waldorf and his similarly wealthy brother, John Jacob V, had to pay taxes in both. In 1919, for example, the two paid $1,134,000 in taxes to the United States and $1,680,000 to Britain, a combined figure that was equal to or even more than the rents they were receiving from the real estate. The orders went out to their New York managers to sell the least profitable of their property. The decision was to sell some of the run-down tenements. The vast property in the Bronx that had been bought by John Jacob Astor III was reduced by the sale of 1,669 lots. William Waldorf's favorite hotel, the Netherlands, was sold, as was the northern half of the old Astor House put up so long before by John Jacob Astor I. The southern half had been torn down some years earlier when the subway was built.

It would be quite a mistake to assume that these sales marked the beginning of the end of the Astor fortune. What was left was the best, and by 1929 the value of the American property had climbed to a hundred million dollars.

In addition to the real estate and stocks and bonds, William Waldorf had left his sons the foundation for a press empire. The Sunday *Observer* had been turned over to Waldorf as early as 1916. In the early 1920's Waldorf and his younger brother, John Jacob Astor V, decided that they wanted to own the influential *Times* of London, too. Abraham Lincoln had said of it some years earlier: "I don't know of anything that has more power, except perhaps the Mississippi." Several of the other British press lords wanted the newspaper, but no one could outbid the Astors with their offer of $6,547,-500.

In 1920 John Jacob V had run for the House of Commons and had lost; the London *Times* had opposed his candidacy. In 1922, as publisher of that influential paper, he was elected as Tory representative of the Dover Division of Kent and succeeded in holding this office for the next twenty-three years.

Although they were fellow publishers, the two brothers were not really close. They visited one another often, but on a somewhat formal basis. Nancy had the gift of irritating her brother-in-law. "It's the press that's always causing the trouble," she remarked one day. "I can't tell you what contempt I have for the press." Waldorf took this sort of comment lightly, but his brother did not. Then, too, John Jacob V was old fashioned and did not think that women belonged in politics.

The five Astor children and their half-brother Robert Shaw must have had mixed feelings about their mother's career. When she was home they all but reeled under the impact of her personality. She took a great, though of necessity occasional, interest in their lives. Each morning when she and they were at home, they were called into her room to join her in "doing the lesson" which consisted of reading passages of the Bible and Christian Science publications. And although Nancy was completely in earnest about her religion, even the "lesson" had to be light in tone. She would talk in a Negro dialect: "Yassir, I'se gonna help yew. Me and Mistah Jesus is gonna help yew." The rest of the children's day, typical of the British upper class of the time, was spent in the care of servants. At five o'clock, bathed and neatly dressed, they joined the grownups once again for the "Children's Hour." Sometimes Waldorf would read to them or Nancy would tell them plantation stories from her Virginia childhood.

Though it sounds delightful, life was not easy for the Astor children because of the character of their parents. Nancy expected and demanded such a high degree of attention and affection that her children found it hard to live up to her. She wanted, and felt it her right, to control their very minds. Her husband, on the other hand, was remote. He felt that his word was final and would not stand any difference of opinion. Still, the children were but one of many responsibilities of the parents. Their eldest son William used to speak most pleasantly of both his parents, but the real warmth in his voice was reserved for his old nurse, Nannie Gibbons. He would stand in front of her portrait and muse: "So kind, so gentle. She was a real influence on us, you see, as Mother and Father were so busy."

As they grew a little older and went away to school, Nancy would visit them periodically, causing them untold embarrassment. She would stop any boy of any age and ask him personal questions: "Have you cleaned your teeth?" On the day after one of her visits, a friend of Michael Astor's admitted that he had heard Lady Astor's voice in the hall and had hidden in a closet until she left. Luckily she was too busy to come very often.

In addition to her political work, she entertained constantly at Cliveden. To name the guests at Cliveden is to give a who's who of half a century. In Cliveden's first and happiest period, royal guests included King Edward VII and, after his death, King George V and Queen Mary, the Archduke Franz Ferdinand of Austria, and the Duchess of Hohenberg. Crown Prince Gustav (now King Gustav VI) of Sweden was such a favored guest that the Astors lent their house in Sandwich for his honeymoon when he married Lady Louise Mountbatten (the aunt of Britain's Prince Philip). Nancy also became friends with the Prince of Wales, who was so briefly to be Edward VIII, and liked to play golf with him. Although Lady Astor was not much of a reader, she liked to have famous authors around. Her opinions on them depended on their social behavior rather than their talent. She declared that James Barrie, author of *Peter Pan,* had been spoiled by success; and Rudyard Kipling, who had written *The Jungle Book,* was a bore, because he sat quietly on the sofa and turned to his wife for moral support whenever he was asked a question.

George Bernard Shaw was the one writer who completely satisfied her demand for fame coupled with wit. The friendship was so complete and long-lasting that many people believe she was the model for the heroine of his plays, *Candida,* and *Saint Joan.*

Shaw introduced Nancy to a strange person to whom she was instantly drawn—Lawrence of Arabia. After leading the Arabs in their battle against Turkey, Lawrence had returned to England. Possibly embittered by his failure to bring about Arab independence, he withdrew from public life and enlisted in the Royal Air Force under the name of T. E. Shaw. Lawrence often left his barracks of an evening to make a swift run on his motorcycle to the Astors' home. Stopped for returning late to quarters one night, Lawrence explained that he had been kept too long at dinner with Lord and Lady Astor and George Bernard Shaw; his fellow soldiers only laughed at him. Sometimes Lawrence would take Nancy riding on his motorcycle, a rare mark of favor.

The only people allowed to fall short of Nancy's high social requirements for guests were those whom she felt were "good." A Christian Science practitioner, automatically "good," was included in almost every group.

On the other hand, she would not dream of inviting anyone she considered to be "bad."

Mahatma Gandhi, the great Indian leader, attracted Nancy by his exceptional purity. At that time the British ruled India, but Gandhi convinced Nancy that India should be independent. He was, thereafter, very much at home with her. Lady Astor's British friends, who believed England should continue to hold a large empire, were surprised one day to enter her drawing room and find Gandhi sitting on the floor turning a spinning wheel.

Throughout her career in Parliament, Nancy believed that people with different political ideas would find ways of cooperating if only they could meet one another. Her reputation was such that sworn enemies came to her parties, but the results she hoped for seldom followed.

She took the problems of Plymouth, which she represented in Parliament, to heart, and with Waldorf's approval, gave many gifts to the city. Social centers for children were opened and houses for workmen built.

Nancy was not content to devote her energies to the problems of Plymouth, women's rights, and drunkenness. She wanted to be a world power, influencing government policy. Gradually the first signs began to appear that Nancy might be getting in over her head when it came to world politics. She did not approve of the Russian Communist government, but her idea of what to do about it was incredibly naïve. In 1925 she offered to pay all expenses for any family foolish enough to want to spend two years in Russia. It was hardly surprising that an Englishman took her up on it, and after traveling at the Astors' expense, returned saying Russia was wonderful.

George Bernard Shaw was invited to Moscow in 1931 and obtained invitations for Lord and Lady Astor and their son David. Shaw was very popular in Russia and was received everywhere, and the Astors followed along after him. Waldorf, as was his way, kept quiet, but Nancy made some remarks that she was never able to live down, even though she later claimed that some of them were falsely reported.

"Now tell me honestly, wouldn't you rather not have had a revolution at all?" she is supposed to have asked Maxim Litvinoff, a high official.

Litvinoff replied solemnly: "My whole life was spent in preparing for one."

When introduced to Premier Josef Stalin, her question was even more tactless: "When will you stop killing people?"

In her own description of their interview she reported that Stalin had asked how England had built such a magnificent empire. Nancy had informed him that the English character was formed by the Bible and that Russia might be just as great if the people returned to religion. Shaw unkindly said that she had made up this entire conversation.

Despite having annoyed the Communists, Nancy returned home to find herself under attack for being a Russian sympathizer. Shaw was making pro-Russian speeches, and in newspaper stories the Astors were included. It was Lady Astor's first taste of unfavorable publicity.

Her attitudes toward Hitler and Mussolini were soon to bring her far worse publicity. By the early 1930's Adolf Hitler and the Nazis were in power in Germany and Benito Mussolini and the Fascist party were ruling Italy. In that period before World War II, some people believed that it would be possible to get along with these dictators. One might have thought that Lady Astor, with her Bible and her devotion to the good, would have been violently against Hitler and Mussolini from the start. But the choice did not appear clear cut to her at all. "The worst thing a human being can do is hate," she said many times and this, the cornerstone of her philosophy, meant opposition to the mass hatred that is war. Under any other circumstances this would be a lofty view, but in Europe of the 1930's it meant tolerating the concentration camps and organized brutality of the Nazis and Fascists.

The bestial treatment of minority groups did not really affect Nancy very much. Nancy possessed all the prejudices of her class, just as did her great-aunt, *the* Mrs. Astor. But the effect of Caroline Astor's prejudices, unpleasant though they were, was relatively harmless. Nothing but the feelings were hurt by a snub, by a refusal of the invitations committee to the Patriarchs. But the same prejudices in Nancy's strife-filled world of the 1930's involved giving silent approval to the imprisonment, torture, and murder of these socially unacceptable Jews. Nancy was so indifferent to what was going on that she said anti-Nazi feeling in the United States was whipped up only by Jews and Communists.

Germany withdrew from the League of Nations in 1933; Lady Astor felt that it must be brought back, no matter what the cost. She went on to urge Britain to disarm, on the principle that Germany would then follow the example and reduce its army, too. Nancy was not alone in this view; many government officials agreed.

The guest list at Cliveden became top heavy with Conservatives, ready to do anything to keep the peace. Visitors included Sir Samuel Hoare, who agreed to let the Italians take over Ethiopia in 1935; Sir John Simon and Lord Edward Halifax, who refused to oppose Hitler; and Neville Chamberlain, the prime minister who signed the Munich Pact, allowing Hitler to grab a large piece of Czechoslovakia. An even less appealing element of the British Fascist movement, headed by Sir Oswald Mosely, also sipped tea in the beautiful drawing rooms of Cliveden. And if that were not enough, Hitler's ambassador, Joachim von Ribbentrop, was invited to dinner with the Astors. Nancy, completely missing the point, felt that she had done all that could possibly have been expected of her as a representative of virtue when Von Ribbentrop greeted her with the Nazi salute and she tossed back: "Stop that nonsense with me."

The only member of the Astor family who disagreed with her was her young son David. He had traveled in Germany in 1931 and had seen a Nazi parade. To his horror he observed that the sidestreets were lined with truckloads of police armed with clubs to use on anyone who objected to the marchers. From then on he was against the Nazis. His parents, however, did not listen to him.

As the Astors owned both the *Times* and the *Observer,* they had two highly influential newspapers in which to express their opinions. Both held to the line that Hitler must and could be soothed. *Time* magazine in America reported that the pro-German propaganda in the London *Times* was "a great deal better than Dr. Paul Joseph Goebbels and the (German) Ministry of Propaganda could turn out."

In 1937 a newspaperman named Claud Cockburn made a bitter attack on the Astor policies in a minor news bulletin, *This Week.* Cockburn accused the Astors, together with the editors of the *Times* and the *Observer* and the Conservative statesmen who were their friends, of plotting to give Hitler anything he wanted. They were in effect ruling the country, he wrote; as Britain's "Second Foreign Office," they were responsible for a pro-German policy. He gave the Astors and their friends the name, "the Cliveden Set." *This Week* was one of the least important or influential of newspapers, if such it could even be called, but major newspapers all over the world picked up its story. The label "Cliveden Set" was fastened onto the Astors and could not be removed no matter how they struggled.

Waldorf wrote a letter to the *Times:* "It is absurd to

associate Cliveden with conspiracies for any particular set of views."

Nancy wrote in a similar way to the *Herald*. Both continued to deny throughout their lives that there was ever such a thing as a Cliveden Set.

And yet, of course, there *was* a Cliveden Set. It did not have quite the degree of power described by Cockburn and his fellows, ("I am supposed to have more power than had Queen Elizabeth, Marie Antoinette, and Cleopatra combined," commented Nancy wryly), but its members unquestionably influenced the thinking of the government. They were the closest friends of the country's highest officials. In addition, the Astors were actually in the government themselves; in 1935 five of them were sitting in the House of Commons— Lady Astor and her son William, her son-in-law Willoughby de Eresby, John Jacob Astor V, and a nephew, Ronald Tree, in addition to Lord Astor in the House of Lords.

Nancy, by personality a leader of this Cliveden set, had the opportunity to do the good she so constantly sought through Christian Science, and she bungled it— without ever knowing she had. When her old enemy Winston Churchill described the Munich Pact as a defeat, she remarked "Nonsense." She visited the United States and declared fiercely: "I abhor Hitler and Hitlerism." But she still urged that war be avoided by coming to terms with him.

The declaration of war with Germany in 1939 brought all such talk and thinking to an abrupt end. Lady Astor threw herself into the war effort, as did the entire Astor family. A Canadian war hospital was again set up on the Cliveden estate. The Astor sons entered the armed forces and served with valor. In his fifties and with only one leg, John Jacob V staunchly took his place as lieutenant colonel with the Fifth Battalion of the City of London Home Guards. Nancy and Waldorf devoted themselves principally to Plymouth, which elected them as Mayoress and Mayor. Nancy remained in Plymouth during the war, setting a fine example for the inhabitants during the bombings. Danger and excitement brought out the best in her. Careless of attacks from the air, she went from shelter to shelter during air raids. As the months went by, Lady Astor arranged for public open-air dances to be held to cheer everyone up. And she, in her sixties, but still light on her feet, danced with the sailors and townspeople.

Toward the end of 1944, with a new Parliamentary election coming up, Lady Astor announced that she would not run again. Her husband had talked her into this decision. He recognized that her political reputation had been hurt by her pro-German policies before the war, and she was not likely to win an election.

The return to private life was hard for Nancy to endure. "I am an extinct volcano," she moaned. But it was not really true. She continued to take the center of the stage wherever she went. When she came to America in 1946, the *New York Times* reported her arrival: "Then Lady Astor, followed by the almost unnoticed Viscount, went to the less-cold waiting room of an adjoining pier where the newsreel men had set up their cameras."

Six years later, as quietly as he had lived, Waldorf died, and the Cliveden period of Nancy's life was over. Lord Astor had given Cliveden to the National Trust, a government body in charge of historic homes, in 1942. The house and grounds were opened to the public on certain days. Waldorf left a fund to pay for upkeep, provided that he and his heirs could continue to live there. But Lady Astor did not wish to remain at Cliveden as a widow. Her son, William, who had inherited the title of viscount, moved in and Nancy moved out and bought a new house in London.

Physically she had not changed too much since the days when she had exchanged insults with Churchill, remaining slim, trim, and pretty. On her eightieth birthday she was still able to play golf. "It's wonderful to be so aged and yet so agile," she told an astonished reporter. But an unaccustomed mood of sadness took over: "Years ago I thought that old age would be dreadful because I would not be able to do the things I want to do. Now I find there is nothing I want to do after all."

She died only days before her eighty-fifth birthday in May of 1964. A few months earlier she appeared on a television show. The interviewer asked her: "Do you believe in God?"

"I think that question's an insult," replied Lady Astor with considerable heat. "Do you think I'm a half-wit?"

8

Modern American Astors

THERE WERE TWO half brothers, and the older one had many millions of dollars and the younger had only a few million dollars. The poorer of the two hated the richer, and to this day says bitterly: "He robbed me of my birthright." The richer brother, who is dead now, hated the poorer one just as much, calling him a wastrel, unfit to handle the fortune that had been handed down from generation to generation. The older one died childless and the money passed out of the American Astor family after more than a century and a half.

The hatred between the two was the almost inevitable result of the will left by their father at the time of his sudden death. When John Jacob Astor IV went down on the *Titanic,* his daughter Alice inherited a trust fund of five million dollars. The same amount went to the lovely young widow, and a three million dollar trust fund for the child she was carrying. All the rest of the money, $69 million, went to his son Vincent. As John

Jacob Astor VI, the child born after his father's death, grew up, he felt the injustice of having received only three million dollars from the father who had given the other son a fortune. The fact that their sister had received little more did not soothe John. "The Astors always favor sons financially over daughters," he points out, convinced that their father would have changed the will after his second son was born. There is obviously no way of knowing what John Jacob IV would have done had he lived. It is, therefore, certainly natural for John to feel that Vincent had cheated him and just as natural for Vincent to have disliked hearing this. He was, after all, following his father's will to the letter.

John did not help his own cause by his way of life. Working only briefly, he has devoted most of his time to enjoying the money he had, which would have seemed a fortune to anyone but an Astor. He has spent it freely on travel, romantic attachments, and buying cars and houses. Vincent, almost old enough to be John's father, was intensely irritated by this.

Vincent himself was a curious mixture of the extravagant rich man and the do-gooder. Already owning thirty cars, he bought a six-thousand-dollar-racer which could go a hundred miles per hour, an incredible speed for the period. At one weekend house party where he had been asked not to bring a valet, he appeared at breakfast without his shoes. He had been unable to get the shoe-trees out of them all by himself. On the other hand, he declared: "It is my duty to show my gratitude (for my fortune) by taking an interest in great public movements and in every way to attempt to aid mankind."

Still, as the violence of his hatred for his young brother shows, his great wealth affected his character. He became an extremely difficult and self-centered person.

"It is hard to be so rich," says a man who knew Vincent Astor well. "His friends were wealthy, but not on the same level. Most people wanted something from him. Even if they had money themselves, they welcomed a free six-month trip on his yacht. Businessmen hoped he would invest in their enterprises and politicians wished for campaign contributions. Vincent saw this and it made him suspicious of everyone, particularly his family. What could his relatives do right? If they ignored him, that was wrong. If they were nice to him, he wondered if they were after something in his will."

Vincent's dark view of humanity was deepened by the unhappiness and coldness he met in his early life. Son of the loveless marriage of Ava and John Jacob Astor IV, Vincent realized when very small that his mother could hardly bear the sight of him. As a result of this rejection, he gave all his affection to his father. John Jacob loved the boy in his way, but really had no idea of how to bring up a child. Until he was twelve, Vincent was left pretty much to the care of first an Irish nurse and then a German governess. He was terribly lonely, because his parents considered very few children well bred enough to be acceptable as playmates. Alice was no company for him, because she was not born until he was ten and she was whisked off to Europe by their mother a few years later. His father was sometimes very severe and when Vincent misbehaved would hit him with a shoe or a strap or send him to bed with a glass of milk instead of dinner. Such severity was alternated with extreme permissiveness. On his eleventh birthday, John gave Vincent permission to drive a car alone around the family estate at Rhinebeck, New York. When Vincent entered St. George's school in Newport, R.I., the other side of John Jacob's nature took over and the boy was given the miserly allowance of fifty cents a week, to be cut to thirty-five cents if his marks were low or his behavior poor.

As Vincent grew up, his odd appearance increased his unhappiness. He was described as looking like an "elongated Neanderthal man." The six-foot-four-inch tall body was thin and hollow chested. His forehead receded and he had a protruding upper lip. He walked with his large feet turned out which, he used to joke, made him feel like a penguin and he adopted this bird as his mascot and trademark. His speech was fast, but rather indistinct, sounding as if he had not quite swallowed something.

From boyhood on Vincent was fascinated by the sea and he wanted to go to Annapolis. His father would not hear of it, and so he entered Harvard.

His college life came to an abrupt end on the April night in 1912 when his father died on the *Titanic*. The reporters gathered at the steamship company office the following morning watched Vincent come out weeping.

The loss of his father was a terrible blow to Vincent and he never quite recovered from it. When John Jacob's body was recovered from the sea, Vincent took the gold watch from the wrist and wore it all his life. But to an Astor, a father's death was more than just a personal matter. The burden was far too great for a young man of twenty. The strain did much to mold his character.

"He has an income of ten thousand dollars a day and can't afford to go to college," wrote *Current Opinion* magazine.

Vincent's youth was cut short. He reacted to this by keeping a childish streak all his life. Twenty years later a friend, asked how Vincent spent his spare time, replied in perfect seriousness: "He liked to play with his model trains. He spent hours and hours with them." A perfect model of a steam train, three feet long, and running on one-quarter mile of tracks, was built for him. Each car was large and solid enough to hold his weight.

Regardless of his age, he would play pranks one day and make sober, considered statements the next. He had an earnest desire to do good with his money. In keeping with this ambition, he ordered a playground built on a Harlem block valued at a million dollars, invited slum mothers and children to go on boatrides, and founded a home for emotionally disturbed children.

Despite the sad example of married life set by his parents, Vincent was married at the age of twenty-two to Helen Dinsmore Huntington. Descended from Samuel Huntington, a signer of the Declaration of Independ-

ence, Helen was a tall, statuesque ash blonde with cool
good looks, perfect grooming, and great poise. Intensely
interested in music—an interest which Vincent did not
share—she played the piano well. Her manner was a
little stiff, concealing a great deal of warmth and kind-
ness. The honeymoon was spent aboard the yacht, where
Vincent was always happiest.

When the United States entered World War I, he
presented his yacht to the government, and encouraged
by his friend, neighbor, and distant relative, Assistant
Secretary of the Navy Franklin Delano Roosevelt, tried
to persuade other yacht owners to do the same. Then he
joined the Navy and served at sea, rising from the rank
of ensign to lieutenant. Helen, never one to sit at home,
went to France where she assisted the Young Men's
Christian Association. Astor's financial contribution was
two million dollars to the Liberty Loan.

With all this war effort, it came, therefore, as quite
a shock to Vincent when a Senate munitions commission later accused him of having made money out of the
war. He denied furiously having had any connection
with companies producing war supplies. But the charge
itself embittered him and increased his feeling that
money was a burden. In time he was to become a
strange, moody man who carried his millions as if they
were a heavy weight on his back, while—and here is the
contradiction in Vincent's character—demanding the
attention and admiration that they brought him.

Even when young, Astor took his position as head of
the family with great seriousness and was exasperated

by his stepmother's behavior as he was in time to be by her son's. One day Madeleine went shopping for her infant son and came home with an ermine wrapper and muff that cost her $230. By the time John Jacob VI was three, Madeleine had run through nearly six thousand dollars on just his clothes and toys. Although she was extravagant, she was not really interested in money. She married William L. Dick in 1918, even though her first husband's will had ordered that she would lose her five-million-dollar trust fund and the use of the Astors' magnificent house at 840 Fifth Avenue, if she remarried.

John Jacob's first wife, the beautiful Ava, did just the same thing the following year when she gave up her divorce settlement to marry Lord Ribblesdale, a widower and former lord-in-waiting to Queen Victoria. Ava was rather disappointed in this marriage, too, as Lord Ribblesdale announced that he was weary of society. He took her off to his country estate and read the classics to her in the evenings with his magnificent bass voice. Party-loving Ava found this excessively boring.

Vincent's sister, Alice, had remained with her mother, although domineering Ava was no more loving as a mother than as a wife. Alice's childhood was, if anything, harder than Vincent's. She was not the great beauty that Ava had been, and still was, but even so, she was a lovely-looking girl. Slightly above the average in height, she had beautiful black hair with blue highlights, brooding eyes, and a soft mouth with a slightly discontented droop that added to its attractiveness. Her voice had a little lilt in it that was particularly winning.

She was seventeen when her mother remarried, and Lord Ribblesdale did little at that date to provide his stepdaughter with a feeling of warmth and belonging. She saw her brother only occasionally, when their mother decided to visit America.

Vincent and Helen by then had moved into *the* Mrs. Astor's old home, which again became a center for New York society. The enormous rooms were still crammed with a museum's worth of paintings, marble sculptures, tapestries, ornaments, gilt, marble, and paneling, all in the spirit of *the* Mrs. Astor's formal era.

The Astors also spent much time at Ferncliff, the estate built by *the* Mrs. Astor's husband William, and at Newport. Ferncliff, where he is now buried, is the place Vincent loved best and he was determined to be an influence for good in the surrounding community. He was horrified one night to look through the windows and see in the distance the white-sheeted, ghostlike figures of members of the Ku Klux Klan lighting a fiery cross. This was one of their ways of terrorizing members of minority groups, chiefly Negroes. Without hesitation Vincent ran into the midst of the hysterical group, stamped out the fire, and told everyone to go home. His dignity was such that they did.

In Newport, Vincent and Helen had inherited Beechwood and the social reputation of *the* Mrs. Astor. Along with many of the other Newport gentlemen, Vincent kept his yacht anchored and ready to carry him off to New York or on a cruise any time boredom or business demanded.

The pattern of business life was at last changing for the Astors. For a century the family had bought real estate and had rented it. They hardly ever sold a piece of property. But this policy was abandoned altogether, as Vincent sold, sold, and sold again. In just about ten years, he disposed of roughly half of his real estate. He received about $40 million for property that had been valued at $31.5 million when his father died.

Even the Waldorf-Astoria, owned jointly by Vincent and his English cousins, was at last put up for sale. Each branch of the family received $7,560,000 in payment for land that had seemed overpriced when William B. Astor had bought it a hundred years earlier for $25,000. The new owners operated the Waldorf-Astoria for four years and then sold it at a handsome profit so that the Empire State Building could be built on that site. The wreckers moved in and tore down the splendid old hotel. An auction of furnishings was held and sandwiches were sold for twenty cents apiece in the Palm Garden where Boldt had once dreamed of serving *the* Mrs. Astor an "unprofitable cup of water." It was the end of an era. Still, when a new hotel arose, it bore the illustrious name again.

Despite all the sales, the Astor hold on New York real estate was not yet at an end. Vincent added to, as well as subtracted from, the total, putting up apartment houses and buying land in Manhattan, the Bronx, and Long Island.

Vincent, at twenty-eight, was already a director of such huge companies as Western Union, American Express, Illinois Central and Great Northern Railroads. He invested in a great many firms, but confessed that his favorite was the Roosevelt Steamship Company, which became the basis for the International Mercantile Marine. "Shipping is about the only business that's still got romance in it," declared Vincent boyishly.

Particularly when young, Vincent was able to leave his business worries in the office. In the evenings he liked to play chess and listen to the radio. A friend telephoned a few minutes after seven o'clock one evening and was told by the butler that Vincent was out, but would be back at seven-fifteen. After the same thing had happened on several occasions, the friend asked Astor just where he went at that time each night. Vincent laughed and admitted that he was really at home—he even changed dinner appointments in order to be there—listening to his favorite nightly radio program. He seldom heard music, although it was his wife's consuming interest. Helen served as director of the New York Philharmonic-Symphony Society and of the Metropolitan Opera Association and later helped to found the New York City Center of Music and Drama. For all their differences, they respected one another and got along well.

It was to Helen that Vincent's sister Alice turned when she fell in love. Her mother, Lady Ribblesdale, had intended to marry Alice to a fabulously rich man and was furious when the girl's choice was Prince Serge Obolensky-Neledinsky-Meletzky. Although Prince Serge could trace his lineage back eleven hundred years to

Rurik, Grand Duke of Novgorod and Kiev, his family's wealth had been lost in the Russian Revolution, and that settled it for Ava. She tried to distract Alice with a series of dashing young men, among them Helen Astor's brother. Despite her brother's candidacy, Helen favored the romantic match with Obolensky and encouraged the young couple to meet at the house she maintained in Paris.

As soon as Alice was twenty-one, she married Prince Serge, and the following year gave birth to a son, Ivan. Waldorf Astor was asked to be a godfather. Serge and Alice considered London to be their home, and only occasionally visited Vincent and Helen in America.

By the mid-1920's Vincent had decided that the Fifth Avenue townhouse built for his grandmother was out of date, and so he sold it. Descendants of the first "four hundred" gathered in the ballroom for a farewell ball. As was the way at Astor parties from the earliest days on, the mayor of New York, this time James J. Walker, attended. In another city or country the building would have survived as a landmark, but in New York a building is used and destroyed. The house and land were sold for three-and-one-half million. Today the Temple Emanu-El stands in that place.

A new house for Vincent was put up at 130 East Eightieth Street. Vincent's attachment to his father was so sentimental that he ordered the bedroom of John Jacob IV to be reproduced and then had the bathroom fixtures transferred. Only the bath tub, an oversized marble creation, was different. Years later when the house was being remodeled to serve as a clubhouse for the Junior League of New York, workmen were unable to move this enormous tub. Clearly installed before the building had been completed, it was too large to go out through any of the doors. In the end it was chopped to bits and sold for marble dust. A cherub that once rested on the soapdish alone remains, standing in the garden.

In Vincent's day a visit to one of his luxurious homes might be an ordeal. The childish streak in his nature found an outlet in practical jokes. Some were simple, such as having the servant waiting on table spill coffee over a guest or call him names. But being rich, Vincent did not need to limit himself to this kind of humor, nor did he do so. His elaborate preparations for a joke often began long before the scheduled visit. One well-to-do businessman joined Vincent for a cruise on his yacht. When the yacht was three days out at sea, a stock market report came through on Vincent's wireless set: the guest's stocks were falling in value. He spent the next few days in black despair, as each report, worse than the one before, revealed that he was utterly ruined. Back on dry land, he discovered that he had been a victim of one of his host's favorite jokes. Astor had prepared by getting an exact list of his friend's holdings.

Vincent's sense of humor did not extend to his young half brother, who spent a weekend or two with him each year and always succeeded in annoying him. John simply would not act in the way that Vincent considered suitable for an Astor. In school his marks were poor, even though he was fairly intelligent.

Vincent was also angry with Alice, who asked for a divorce only five years after having defied her mother and battled her way to a romantic marriage with her prince. Vincent considered divorce a sign of weak character and urged them to make up.

Although Vincent and Alice had always gotten along, they never really understood one another. Her whims and careless way with money irritated him, even when she was not threatening divorce. While staying in New York, she would suddenly get the idea of visting him at Ferncliff and would immediately set off in a taxi, even though she owned a car and employed a chauffeur. Her extravagance was so well known that a story went the rounds that she had bought a New York City taxicab for her use, allowing the driver to pick up other fares when she did not need him. It was quite useless for anyone to argue with Alice, who simply would not listen.

She did not listen to Vincent's objections to her divorce, either, and went to Nevada in the summer of 1932. Shortly after the divorce became final, Alice made the second of her four marriages, to Raimund von Hofmannsthal, an Austrian writer. They went to Europe where Alice became a noted patron of the arts and devoted much of her portion of the Astor fortune to supporting a ballet company and other artistic ventures.

To make clear his position on her divorce, Vincent promptly offered Obolensky a job in the Astor Estate office, invited him on the cruises of the *Nourmahal,* and considered him an intimate friend.

Vincent found his friends easier to get along with

than his family. One of the closest friendships of his life was with Franklin Delano Roosevelt. After his paralyzing attack of poliomyelitis, Roosevelt used to come to Ferncliff and exercise in the swimming pool. The two men with neighboring estates came from the same background—Roosevelt was a great-nephew of the Franklin Delano who had married Laura Astor—and they understood one another. Both took wealth and the power that goes with it for granted, and both had a sense of mission. Although Vincent lacked the brilliance, direction, drive, and charm that carried Roosevelt into the White House, he shared the desire to do something worthwhile with his life.

"It is unreasonable to suppose that because a man is rich, he is also useless," Vincent declared, perhaps a little wistfully.

No Astor could be ignored by politicians and first one political party and then the other tried to convince him that the most useful thing he could do would be to devote at least a bit of his riches to them. As a young man he had been a Republican and had contributed to the campaign fund of Warren Gamaliel Harding in 1920 and to Calvin Coolidge in 1924. Soon afterwards he met Herbert Lehmann, later to be governor of New York, and William H. Woodin, who became Secretary of the Treasury. Both men were Democrats and influenced Astor to change parties. In 1928 he contributed to Al Smith's ill-fated Presidential campaign and four years later supported Roosevelt in his successful race for the Presidency.

Roosevelt often joined Vincent on his yacht. Astor had a special ramp built so that Roosevelt's wheelchair could be taken directly on board. The *Nourmahal* was the size of a small ocean liner and could cross the Atlantic in nine days. It had been built in Germany in the late 1920's for about a million dollars, taken in part from the sale of his old yacht. One man had agreed to buy that yacht if Vincent would pay him five thousand dollars for his orangutang Freda, which he loved but could not care for. This was just the kind of idea that Vincent appreciated and he took the ape. Its former owner then decided that he did not want a yacht anyway. Vincent took Freda home, nonetheless, and she became known as "Mrs. Astor's pet orangutang." After four years the delight of having such a pet wore thin, and Freda was presented to the Bronx Zoo where she promptly relieved her keeper of his broom and then turned his hose on him. The new yacht which had indirectly brought Freda into Astor's life had three decks, one with spaces for guns to be mounted on it, a pine-paneled library, a number of lounges, a walnut-paneled dining room where eighteen people could sit comfortably at table, and an emergency operating room.

A month before his inauguration, President-elect Roosevelt took a ten-day vacation trip aboard the *Nourmahal* with Astor. Having Vincent's up-to-date wireless equipment at his disposal, he was not completely cut off from Washington. He kept in constant touch with Raymond Moley, who was a key member of the group of advisers who were to be called the "Brain Trust." Moley was forming the Cabinet, and Vincent felt himself to be in on the making of history.

The *Nourmahal* landed at Miami, Florida, where Roosevelt was to address a political rally. A procession of cars set off for Bayfront Park, with Roosevelt in the front one and Vincent two cars behind. When the President-elect, who had been helped to the top of the rear seat of his car, began to address the crowd, Vincent had a sudden premonition of disaster.

"Why, anyone in the crowd could stand back and shoot Roosevelt!" he exclaimed.

In the crowd at that very moment was Guiseppe Zangara, a bricklayer and stonemason who hated all presidents. He had thought of going to Washington and attacking President Herbert Hoover, but had decided the cold climate would aggravate his stomach trouble. Now the President-elect had come to him in Florida. Zangara raised his arm and took aim. The shots rang out, but luckily Roosevelt had dropped down to his seat when he finished speaking and escaped injury.

The scene was bloody, nonetheless, as the bullets struck and killed Mayor Anton Cermak of Chicago and wounded four people in the crowd. Zangara, who never had a chance of escaping, was seized and placed on the trunk rack of the car in which Astor was riding. One policeman held the assassin while another perched on the running broad. One of the injured men was put inside the car. Vincent held his head, put a cigarette in his mouth, and tried to soothe him. The wounded man could only mutter over and over again that his wife would not be able to get home, as the car keys were in his pocket.

When they finally arrived at the hospital, they met Roosevelt coming out. Vincent thought that the future President appeared shaken and talked him into coming back to spend the night quietly on the *Nourmahal*.

After Roosevelt's inauguration he immediately presented a bold and far-reaching program in an effort to lift the economy out of the Great Depression. He reorganized the banks, reduced the amount of gold backing the dollar, created the Civilian Conservation Corps to train and employ young men, began public-works programs and farm relief, and proposed the Tennessee Valley Authority to develop the Tennessee River basin. And Vincent was there on the inside, close to the President, a trusted friend, just as on the other side of the Atlantic, his English relatives were close to the policy makers of Europe.

Vincent wanted to take a more active part himself, even though he knew he was not suited for a life in politics. For one thing, he suffered from stagefright whenever he had to make a speech. At least he could copy the British Astors and purchase a newspaper. At that time W. Averell Harriman, who was later to be governor of New York and ambassador at the Vietnam peace talks in Paris, and his sister, Mrs. Mary Rumsey, were also in the market. They had asked Raymond Moley, who was then Assistant Secretary of State, if he would edit whatever publication they bought. Although Harriman came from the same background of wealth and privilege as the Astors and Roosevelts, he and Vincent never liked one another. And once Astor took a dislike to anyone, he became impossible to deal with. "No one could be more charming if he liked you," remembers another member of that set, "or more unattractive if he did not."

Still, it seemed the wise move for them to pool their efforts, and the Harrimans' choice of Moley as editor was the very thing to win Vincent over. Moley was the type of person whom Astor admired—gentlemanly, intellectual, intelligent, hard-working, and the close friend of great men. Being fond of Moley, Vincent showed only his charming side.

"I heard other people complain that Vincent was a tough man," says Moley, "but never to me."

In fact, Moley was the only person whom Astor could stand seeing in the early morning, a time of day when he hated the whole world.

Astor and the Harrimans decided to start a news magazine instead of buying a newspaper. It would compete with Henry Luce's ten-year-old *Time* and Thomas J.C. Martyn's newborn *News-Week*. When they told Roosevelt about their plans, he said he would be their first subscriber and gave them one dollar on the spot. The Harrimans agreed to put up $125,000 apiece and Vincent matched them with $250,000, and the first issue of *Today* appeared in October of 1933. On a cold December day of the following year Mary Rumsey went riding. Her horse threw her and she was killed. Vincent, who had never liked being only half owner, took over

Mary's share in the enterprise and became the dominant partner. Some time afterward *News-Week,* in serious financial trouble, was bought and merged with *Today.* The joint magazine was called *Newsweek,* dropping the hyphen. It was fortunate for *Newsweek* that Vincent was never one to accept failure. He supported the magazine throughout the depression. In the nine years that it took *Newsweek* to begin to make money, Vincent spent five million dollars on it.

Although Roosevelt was the first subscriber, *Today* and then *Newsweek* did not support his policies for very long. Moley broke with Roosevelt early, resigning from the Cabinet, and leaving the Brain Trust, and he criticized the Administration vigorously in the magazine. Vincent was one of Roosevelt's close friends, but he did not ask Moley to be kinder.

In 1935 Astor urged Roosevelt to take a vacation on his yacht, pointing out that the *Nourmahal* was always ready to take off at a moment's notice. It cost Vincent $125,000 a year to keep the crew on broad and the ship in perfect condition. Roosevelt replied that if the rich could afford such unnecessary extravagance, perhaps it was time to "soak the rich." Taxes were greatly increased. Although the "Soak the Rich" tax program affected Vincent financially, contrary to most reports, he remained on good terms with Roosevelt personally. Vincent was always intensely loyal to the few people he really liked.

These, to be sure, did not include the half brother who had by then come of age and into possession of his trust fund. On July 1, 1934, John Jacob Astor VI made the first of his three marriages, this one to Ellen Tuck French in one of the great weddings of society history. The *New York Times* considered the event important enough for front page coverage and gave almost a full page farther back to the details. No mention was made of the fact that Vincent had not attended.

Seven months after the wedding, John, aged twenty-two, decided it was time to go to work. In the depths of the depression Vincent was the only person who would give him a job. Vincent had him taken on by the International Mercantile Marine Company for twenty-five dollars a week. John was shifted from job to job within the company in order to learn the business from the ground up. His first assignment was on the piers and after that he was moved to the main office. John stuck it out for a year and a half and then quit. "I felt I wasn't getting anywhere," he explains. And considering how Vincent hated him, that is very likely. The die was cast. From then on Vincent was convinced that John was just a playboy.

To make their relationship even more difficult, it turned out to be John, not Vincent, who fathered an heir, the only male Astor to carry on the name and tradition of the American Astors. The child was named William. There have been and are any number of Williams in the Astor family; it is second only to John Jacob. But John selected it in honor of his grandfather, husband of *the* Mrs. Astor.

Vincent carried his hatred of John into the next generation. He refused ever to see his nephew.

When his sister had divorced Obolensky, Vincent had asked if he could adopt their son Ivan, but they refused. He seldom thereafter spoke of his own childlessness.

Although Vincent was the first Astor to possess a fortune and have no son to leave it to, he did not neglect his business interests. *Newsweek* and the St. Regis Hotel built by his father were his favorite enterprises. He supervised every detail of the management of the St. Regis himself. He threw himself into the planning with boyish enthusiasm as if it were a new toy to add to his model trains. His friends were buttonholed and earnestly asked what kind of mustard they liked and how thick a slice of roast beef should be. Members of the staff were sent to the great hotels of Europe to learn from their example.

He appreciated good food, although he never ate heavily, and the same table was reserved for him in the Oak Room of the St. Regis every day. He was far too practical to let it stay empty if he were not going to be there, and would telephone the headwaiter before the lunchtime rush and tell him to give the place to someone else.

"Mr. Astor had no children; the St. Regis was his baby. He loved it," says Pierre Bultinck, who managed the hotel for him for seventeen years.

During the 1930's Vincent gave almost the same kind of loving care to the luxury apartments he owned, worrying about garbage disposal, elevator service, and the selection of doormen. He kept an apartment and office for himself at 120 East End Avenue, and in order to improve the neighborhood around it bought up those nearby tenements that he did not already own and had them rebuilt.

Unlike his forebears, he refused to leave all improvement of his property to sublandlords, but upgraded them himself. Along with this change came another and more basic one: The tenements which had brought wealth to his father, grandfather, and great-grandfather at last passed out of Astor hands. The mayors of New York had talked piously of clearing up the terrible slums, from the middle of the nineteenth century on. It was not until Fiorello H. LaGuardia took office in the 1930's that forthright action was taken. A Tenement House Department was established in the New York Housing Authority and a great deal of attention was paid to the slums. Every time a tenement fire broke out —and there were many, as always—the newspapers would describe it in great detail. Attacks on conditions in the tenements were made repeatedly. Vincent was more affected by public opinion than his ancestors had been, and he was not planning to leave the country as William Waldorf had done. Then, too, he had a desire to do good. And so Astor decided to offer most of his remaining tenements to the Housing Authority, and he told the Commissioner to pay any price he thought fair. Vincent received $189,281, which was considerably less than the value of the land alone. The buildings were in such terrible condition, though, that a third of them had to be torn down and the others were rebuilt. Astor sold some more of his property, improved other parts of it, and as his forebears might have warned him, he was "landlord of New York" no more.

But real estate had never meant as much to him as to earlier generations of his family.

"The sea was the great love of his life," according to one of the people who knew him best. "Whatever else is said about Vincent, that cannot be left out. The only books he really liked were sea stories or naval histories. He knew the name and the size of every ship afloat in the Navy anywhere."

Several months of every year were spent cruising the waters of the world on the *Nourmahal*. He often combined his greatest pleasure, the life at sea, with a dream that he might make at least a small mark as a scientist.

"If you label a man as a scientist, he is instantly accepted by the public mind as a more than ordinarily useful person," said Astor sadly. "If you label a man as a lawyer or give him any professional tag, the public mind associates him with worth-while achievement. But if you say of a man that he is merely rich, he is immediately docketed as a wealthy wastrel and whatever he attempts to do to show that he is a sincere well-wisher of his fellow men is either discounted or misinterpreted on account of his wealth."

Many of the cruises became scientific expeditions and he invited leading scientists to come along. With their guidance, he collected specimens of rare fish off the Galapagos Islands in the Pacific Ocean west of Ecuador, and presented them to the government aquarium at Bermuda. On another trip to the Fiji Islands in the South Pacific, he gathered unusual forms of sea plants and animals. Switching from the serious to the absurd, he had a typical rich man's fancy of transporting Newport lobsters to the waters off Bermuda, where he had a large vacation home. Thirty-six parent lobsters were put in special tanks and the *Nourmahal* set off on its journey; unfortunately, the shellfish died in the heat while the yacht was crusing through the Gulf Stream.

Although it is hard to imagine what an Astor might have done with any more money, Vincent one day set off in search of buried treasure. Like any schoolboy, he was excited by the idea of finding the pirate treasure that was rumored to lie beneath the sands of Cocos Island off the coast of Costa Rica. Upon the *Nourmahal*'s arrival, the Astor party found that other people were also hunting for the gold. Tempers flared to such a pitch that the Costa Rican government sent soldiers to the island to prevent bloodshed—and to claim a share if anyone found the buried hoard. Astor, always sure that he was right, was convinced that he had located the general area of the cache, but failed to find the pirate's gold.

At home Vincent continued to tell everyone that divorce was most disgraceful—for others. But he was divorced after more than a quarter of a century of marriage to Helen and married Mary Benedict "Minnie" Cushing.

World War II took him from the side of his second wife only a year after their marriage. The outbreak of fighting did not surprise him; he had been expecting it since 1928 when he had ordered spaces for guns on the deck of his new yacht. He immediately offered the *Nourmahal* to the government. Although Astor was by then close to fifty, he wanted active service. A captain in the Naval Reserve, he was made a convoy commodore and was assigned to bring war materiel to Europe and wounded men back.

Vincent's rank of captain in the Navy remained his greatest source of pride long after the war and all business associates were careful to address him as "Captain." At one time, when spending a few days in Maine, Astor was enraged that the doorman at the hotel greeted him as "Colonel." He was not at all soothed when old New England hands told him that the doorman had meant to be flattering. In Maine anyone who owns a dinghy is a captain; colonels, on the other hand, are rare.

He never asked for or got the *Nourmahal* back after the war. His friends, noting his increasing gloominess as he grew older, urged him to purchase another yacht, perhaps a smaller one, but he never did. He bought himself an airplane, but clearly never considered it a substitute.

As he grew older Vincent began to think deeply about charity and in 1948 he set up the Vincent Astor Foundation, dedicated to the "alleviation of human misery." The Foundation received many odd requests for money. The Mackinac Island Medical Center asked for a contribution because John Jacob Astor I had once had a trading post there. Vincent's business advisers considered this "the silliest reason to give a grant," but he gave one anyway. And although William Waldorf had declared the Astors free of responsibility for the New York Public Library, Vincent had continued to make donations and to serve as trustee.

Astor liked his wife to take an interest in his favorite projects, and Minnie joined the library's Women's Council and decorated some of the suites at the St. Regis. But the marriage was ill-fated, and in 1953 the man who was strongly against divorce was divorced again. He was later married for the third time to Mary Brooke Marshall, granddaughter of an admiral and daughter of a Marine Corps commander. Like Vincent, Brooke had been married twice before, but unlike him had a married son and twin grandsons.

His own three marriages did not make him more tolerant of his sister's four marriages or his half brother's three. John's second marriage to Gertrude Gretsch had produced a daughter, Mary Jacqueline. But in 1954 he fell madly in love with pretty blonde Dolores "Dolly" Fullman. The infatuated Astor then had the poor judgment to marry Dolly impulsively, even though his divorce from Gertrude was not recognized in most states. Love did not survive marriage and Dolly and John were separated after only six weeks. Nonetheless Dolly refused to give him a divorce for years thereafter. Although John had no one but himself to blame for the awkward position he was left in, this did not make him feel any better about it. John's misfortune did not soften his half brother's heart. The two were not even on speaking terms. If Vincent saw John on the street, he passed without a word.

The Astor Estate underwent changes quite as drastic as those in the personal lives of the Astors during those years. Vincent hired new managers, who reinvested his money in common stocks. As this was done in 1953 when stock market prices were low, just about everything purchased went up.

What was left of the real estate was found to be un-profitable. The income from most of the buildings had dropped to practically nothing. His holdings included some extremely small and unprofitable properties, such as a building with a Nedick's luncheonette and a Regal shoe store on the ground floor and a second floor that was condemned for use.

Astor and his managers began to sell and to make new plans. Vincent came to the office every morning and discussed the suggested sales and purchases. His chief business manager, Allan W. Betts, tried to talk him into giving up the St. Regis.

"Astor would not hear of it. He went there for lunch every day."

At one time Betts suggested that they invest in a real-estate development in Venezuela, but Astor refused flatly. He explained that some years earlier he had been cruising in Latin American waters on the *Nourmahal*. One of the dictators then in power invited Vincent to go shark-fishing. At dawn the following day, just as the party was about to set out, two soldiers led a horse onto the deck. Astor was puzzled, but remained silent. The brutal intention became clear only when the boat entered shark-infested waters. The horse was then thrown overboard, and the dictator and his ministers shot it with machine guns. The sharks, attracted by the blood, swam in and the "fishermen," roaring with glee, shot at them. On the return trip the dictator insisted that one of his cabinet ministers jump overboard and swim to shore. The dictator fired in circles around the man as he swam.

"What better example do you need of a lack of morality?" asked Vincent.

He was getting old and he had the dream of building a group of buildings to be known as Astor Plaza and to be even larger and more famous than Rockefeller Center. He would start by putting up a forty-six-story office building with a heliport on the roof, he announced, at a cost of seventy-five million dollars. But a new era of Astor real estate was not to dawn. Everything went wrong. The land he wanted to use at Park Avenue and Fifty-third Street was owned by the William Waldorf Astor Estate. This, oddly enough, was of no help to him. Vincent and his English cousins were friends and sometimes visited one another, but business was business and the William Waldorf Astor Estate refused to give Vincent a mortgage for the land. His efforts to raise the capital failed because business turned bad in 1957 and 1958 and no one had money to spare. Astor tried to find a bank to act as backer, but none approved of his list of prospective tenants. Behind Vincent's back people called Astor Plaza "Disaster Plaza." Finally in

1958 he was forced to admit that he had failed and the First National City Bank took over the area and put up its own building there. It was the fall of the house of Astor real estate.

Some of Astor's friends felt that he could still have gotten himself out of this predicament if it had not been for his poor health. His circulation was so bad that it was hard for him to walk. Nonetheless, he managed to get around a bit, as a statement by his English cousin, Lord William Astor, shows: "His latter passion was for prolonged and serious games of croquet." It was, of course, the only sport he could still play.

Despite the failure of the Astor Plaza plan, Vincent's fortune had actually grown, because his stocks had greatly increased in value. For all his mistakes with the real estate, he had almost doubled his inheritance, working it up from $69 million to more than $127 million.

When Vincent died at sixty-seven, he left half of this fortune to his widow and half to the Vincent Astor Foundation. This came as a terrible shock to his half brother. John had been brought up on the Astor tradition of money passed from generation to generation. In spite of the feud, he could not believe that Vincent would cut him out of the will altogether. The farthest his imagination could take him was that Vincent might by-pass him and leave the millions to John's son, William, so that the dynasty could go on. But with Vincent's death, the great fortune originated by John Jacob Astor I so long before went out of the American Astor family forever.

"People say that the British Astors are a branch of the family," comments John Astor sadly. "That is no longer true. Today they are the trunk and we the branch."

9

The Astor Legacy

IN THE BEGINNING of the Astor story there was a poor German immigrant with an American dream. He worked hard all his life, believing that any man could get rich in America. And in making himself rich, he helped in the making of a nation.

The fur trade from which young Astor wrested his first fortune was of great importance in opening up Western and Canadian wildernesses. In a search for new markets, he expanded trade between this country and the Orient. Both of these enterprises contributed to the growth of the port of New York.

John Jacob Astor I was the first man to grasp what New York might become and to invest in its future. What is more, he passed his vision on to his children and grandchildren.

No other family has ever owned so much of a modern city—owned it in the most literal sense, too. Countless blocks, thousands of houses, scores of commercial buildings, hotels, miles of waterfront property, acres of vacant lots—all, all belonged to the Astors.

Possession of land and houses led to the possession of power and the family became a major force in both national and city politics. And when some of the Astors moved to the other side of the Atlantic Ocean, they quickly became influential in British politics as well.

Today it would seem that the story of the Astors in America is drawing to an end. Lacking great wealth, power, or public office, their influence has declined.

What is left of the fortune has crossed the ocean to England and it is there that the Astors still hold the power that they had here for so many years. They have been in America seldom since William Waldorf's time. Still, theirs is an American fortune. Their high position is supported by the rents from more than a hundred million dollars' worth of United States real estate.

What does remain of the American side of this family? Its name? "Astor" has become a word as well as a proper noun. John Jacob Astor I, the founder of the Astor fortune, ate his ice cream and peas with a knife, but today his name stands for wealth, power, and social acceptability.

No doubt the legendary Mrs. Astor, who believed—and history has proved her right—that she needed no first name to identify her, has helped to create this image. In the world of society her dream lives on. Many of the very rich to this day follow the way of life that she prescribed so many years ago. It is a life of dancing classes, debuts, and fashionable balls.

In many cities one will find an Astor hotel, club, theater, or—in the case of those attempting to add glamor to the commonplace—garage, luncheonette, or small business.

But the Astors have left a legacy that is far greater than that of social ritual and a famous name. This family has helped to make this country and the city of New York what they are. The Astor imprint is strongly on that city. Riding the New York subway that did so much to increase the value of Astor property half a century ago, one comes to Astor Place. It is no longer the fashionable neighborhood it was when John Jacob I and his son, William Backhouse, stepped heavily out of their front doors to go to the Astor Estate office. This is just as John Jacob would have had it. The city, said Astor, will expand to the north, and houses and office buildings will rise on the cabbage farms of the poor and the country estates of the rich. And he put his energies and his fortune into helping to make this happen.

The real estate owned by the American branch of the family has long since gone. After Vincent Astor's death both *Newsweek* and his favorite St. Regis Hotel were sold. The Astor Hotel in New York has been torn down, and the old Astor Library, the one big charity of John Jacob Astor I, has been transformed into a theater.

But though all the landmarks go or are changed beyond recognition, what remains is the most important. John Jacob Astor's vision of New York *is* New York.

THE ASTOR LINE OF DESCENT

The Astor fortune and real estate were passed down from Astor father to Astor sons for many generations. This is the main line of descent:

John Jacob Astor (1763–1848)
m. Sarah Todd

William Backhouse Astor (1792–1875) m. Margaret Rebecca Armstrong

William Backhouse Astor, Jr. (1830–1892) m. Caroline Webster Schermerhorn

John Jacob Astor IV (1864–1912) m. 1. Ava Lowle Willing

(William) Vincent Astor (1891–1959) no children
but his father

John Jacob Astor IV had married again
m. 2. Madeleine Talmadge Force

John Jacob Astor VI (1912–
m. Ellen Tuck French

William Backhouse Astor (1935–
m. Charlotte Fisk

William Backhouse Astor, Jr. (1959–

John Jacob Astor III (1822–1890) m. Charlotte Augusta Gibbes

William Waldorf Astor, First Viscount (1848–1919)
m. Mary Dahlgren Paul

(William) Waldorf Astor, Second Viscount (1870–1952)
m. Nancy Langhorne Shaw

William Waldorf Astor, Third Viscount (1907–1966)
m. Sarah K. E. Norton

William Waldorf Astor, Fourth Viscount (1952–

and

Waldorf Astor, Second Viscount had a younger son

John Jacob Astor V, Baron Astor of Hever (1886–
m. Lady Violet Elliot Mercer-Nairne

Gavin Astor (1918–
m. Lady Irene Haig

John Jacob Astor VIII (1946–

Index

Index

Index

Index

Index

Index

Index

Index

Index